Praise for A Royal Commitment

"When I met Prince Manvendra and Prince DeAndre for the first time, I was struck by the devotion and love they had for each other and I was thinking how their love overcame the cultural differences that must have been there and of course the resistance to their marriage in a culture that is still very resistant to the idea of same-sex marriage. They had to go through quite a bit and I would imagine that they still have to deal with the bigotry and ignorance daily, especially being in the public eye by people who are fearful and that's what it comes down to—fear. Their love can change the world, they are an example of what love means. They are quite an inspiration."

~ Belinda Carlisle Mason of the Go-Go's

"Prince Manvendra Singh Gohil—or as I like to refer to him by the more simple moniker, Prince—has been an inspiration and a light to so many people. As if being the world's first ever out gay prince was not enough, he has worked tirelessly to further the rights of fellow LGBTQIA+ Indians and to foster understanding and compassion around HIV/AIDS and queerness in general throughout the world. That he has found love in addition to making such a huge impact and being such a force for good is the perfect icing on the cake for such a gentle and inspiring man's life. I cannot wait to read his memoir and to celebrate Manvendra and his husband DeAndre and whatever great accomplishments and good they achieve in their lives together."

~ Alan Cumming, Scottish Actor

"Having the privilege of knowing HRH Prince Manvendra Singh Gohil since the early 2000s and forming a profound connection with him and his husband (now a dear, close friend), DeAndre is truly priceless to me. Sharing a similar background with Manvendra, including being excommunicated by my family and cut off from my inheritance, has created an unbreakable bond. Through thick and thin, I've always found a 'family' in them. Manvendra serves as an elder brother to whom I can turn whenever I feel low, while DeAndre provides valuable advice and keeps me grounded when needed. Their memoir, *A Royal Commitment: Ten Years of Marriage and Activism*, beautifully captures the essence of their journey and the strength of their love, making their story an inspiration to all. Whether in moments of joy or sorrow, I'm grateful to have two brothers whose story is not only relatable but also serves as a beacon of hope for others."

~ Adam Pasha, Bengaluru's first Drag Queen.

"When two people come together in a commitment to love each other it is always a beautiful thing. The very public romance between Prince Manvendra Singh Gohil and his husband DeAndre Richardson is not just beautiful, it is of significant importance as it challenges entrenched societal norms and fosters greater acceptance and visibility for LGBTQIA+ individuals, particularly in regions where such openness is less common. As a member of royalty in India, Prince Manvendra's willingness to embrace his identity and share his love openly with DeAndre not only empowers others within the LGBTQIA+ community but also serves as a catalyst for broader conversations about equality, representation, and human rights. Their relationship stands as a beacon of hope and inspiration, illustrating the power of love to transcend barriers and ignite positive change on a global scale."

~ Brian Rusch, CEO, Out For Equality

"Change your thinking, change your life, are the values I cultivated from Prince Manvendra and Duke DeAndre. Congratulations on celebrating 10 years of happy married life and commitment to activism. Cheers for many more years of togetherness, happiness, and love. Prince Manvendra and Duke DeAndre are living, international inspirational role models of love, resilience, understanding, compassion, and peace. Our family was blessed to celebrate their 9th wedding anniversary in Columbus, Ohio. Prince Manvendra and Duke DeAndre believe in uplifting our vulnerable populations through education, commitment, empowerment, and bringing about change in our society to accept our children's passions, dreams, happiness, and freedom.

Eyes Open International is grateful to Prince Manvendra for sharing his experience and expertise on the EOI Board of Directors. Once again, congratulations Prince Manvendra and Duke DeAndre on your 10th anniversary and many more. Teamwork makes the Dreamwork."

~ Harold D'Souza, founder of Eyes Open International

A ROYAL COMMITMENT

A ROYAL COMMITMENT

TEN YEARS OF MARRIAGE AND ACTIVISM

**PRINCE MANVENDRA GOHIL
AND
DUKE DEANDRE**

Copyright © 2024 HRH Crown Prince Manvendra Singh Gohil of Rajpipla and HRH Prince DeAndre Duke of Hanumanteshwar. All rights reserved.

No part of this publication shall be reproduced, transmitted, or sold in whole or in part in any form without prior written consent of the author, except as provided by the United States of America copyright law. Any unauthorized usage of the text without express written permission of the publisher is a violation of the author's copyright and is illegal and punishable by law. All trademarks and registered trademarks appearing in this guide are the property of their respective owners.

For permission requests, write to the publisher, addressed "Attention: Permissions Coordinator," at the address below.

Publish Your Purpose
141 Weston Street, #155
Hartford, CT, 06141

The opinions expressed by the Author are not necessarily those held by Publish Your Purpose.

Ordering Information: Quantity sales and special discounts are available on quantity purchases by corporations, associations, and others. For details, contact the author at hanumanteshwar1927@yahoo.com.

Edited by: Elliott Tapia-Kwan, Gillian Rodgerson, Emily Ribeiro
Cover design by: Nelly Murariu
Typeset by: Jet Launch

ISBN: 979-8-88797-988-5 (hardcover)
ISBN: 979-8-88797-989-2 (paperback)
ISBN: 979-8-88797-987-8 (ebook)

Library of Congress Control Number: 2024914581

First edition, October 2024

The information contained within this book is strictly for informational purposes. The material may include information, products, or services by third parties. As such, the Author and Publisher do not assume responsibility or liability for any third-party material or opinions. The publisher is not responsible for websites (or their content) that are not owned by the publisher. Readers are advised to do their own due diligence when it comes to making decisions.

Publish Your Purpose is a hybrid publisher of non-fiction books. Our mission is to elevate the voices often excluded from traditional publishing. We intentionally seek out authors and storytellers with diverse backgrounds, life experiences, and unique perspectives to publish books that will make an impact in the world. Do you have a book idea you would like us to consider publishing? Please visit PublishYourPurpose.com for more information.

Disclaimer

A Royal Commitment: Ten Years of Marriage and Activism is a memoir based on the lived experiences of HRH Prince Manvendra Singh Gohil of Rajpipla and HH Prince DeAndre Duke of Hanumanteshwar. The content of this memoir is a subjective recollection of events, emotions, and perspectives as observed and experienced by the co-authors.

While every effort has been made to present an accurate and authentic account of their journey, it is important to note that memories can be subjective, and interpretations may vary. The memoir reflects the personal experiences, beliefs, and reflections of HRH Prince Manvendra and HH Prince DeAndre at the time of writing.

Readers are encouraged to approach the memoir with an open mind, recognizing that it represents a specific viewpoint and narrative. The co-authors acknowledge that others may have different perspectives on the events and topics discussed in the memoir.

This memoir is intended for personal reflection and entertainment purposes. The co-authors do not assume responsibility for any interpretations or conclusions drawn by readers based on the content presented in the memoir.

The names of individuals, places, and organizations mentioned in the memoir are real, and any resemblance to actual persons, living or dead, or actual events is purely coincidental.

Your understanding and respect for the co-authors' shared experiences are greatly appreciated.

Dedication

To love, the unwavering force that knows no boundaries, defies expectations, and triumphs over adversity.

To our families, whose unwavering support has been the bedrock of our journey.

To the LGBTQIA+ community, whose resilience and courage inspire us daily.

To those who paved the way before us, fighting for the rights and visibility we now cherish.

To every individual navigating the delicate dance between tradition and authenticity.

To the dreamers, the advocates, and those who believe in a world where love knows no prejudice.

This memoir is dedicated to you—all the beautiful souls who understand that commitment is not just a promise to each other but a pledge to make the world a better, more inclusive place.

With love,

DeAndre & Manvendra

Table of Contents

Disclaimer xi
Dedication xiii
Table of Contents xv
Introduction xvii
A Call To Action xix

A Royal Beginning (2013–2015)

Chapter 1: The Beginning of Our Journey (2013) 3
Chapter 2: United in Vows 11
Chapter 3: Navigating Royal Realities 19

The Intersection of Love and Advocacy (2016–2018)

Chapter 4: Voices Unveiled 35
Chapter 5: Love in the Spotlight 41
Chapter 6: Breaking Barriers 51

Expanding Horizons (2019–2020)

Chapter 7: Cultural Connections 67
Chapter 8: Love Knows No Borders 75

The Continuing Journey (2021–2023)

Chapter 9: Reflection on Ten Years 91
Chapter 10: Beyond the Decade 95
Chapter 11: Forever Royal. 109

Afterword 119
Acknowledgments 121
About the Authors 123
A Call To Action. 125
Stay In Touch With Us. 127

Introduction

In the embrace of tradition and the dance of modernity, this memoir unfolds—a testament to a love that transcends boundaries and a commitment that challenges societal norms. Our memoir invites you into the intricacies of a decade-long journey, where a marriage is not only a union of two souls but a profound intersection of royalty and activism.

As you embark on these pages, prepare to be immersed in the rich tapestry of our lives—a tapestry woven with threads of cultural heritage, societal expectations, and the vibrant hues of the LGBTQIA+ spectrum. The pages hold not only the chronicles of our union but also the echoes of a resounding call for change, acceptance, and the celebration of love in all its forms.

The story begins in the corridors of a royal dynasty in India, where tradition and history cast long shadows. Here, against a backdrop of centuries-old customs, we navigate the complexities of marriage, identity, and our roles as advocates for LGBTQIA+ rights. Our memoir is an exploration of the delicate balance between honoring heritage and forging an authentic path—a path that, at times, leads to uncharted territories.

As the narrative unfolds, you will witness the evolution of our lives—a journey marked by triumphs, challenges, and a relentless commitment to making a difference. It extends beyond the private realm of our love, becoming a force that propels us to the forefront of social movements, challenging preconceptions, and inspiring change.

This is more than a memoir; it is an invitation to reflect on the intersections of love, identity, and the transformative power of authenticity. It is a testament to the belief that every love story, regardless of its context, has the potential to reshape the world.

So, step into our world. Experience the echoes of ancient traditions, the resonance of a modern love story, and the call to activism that binds it all together. This memoir is a journey—a journey that mirrors the complexities of our own lives and, in doing so, invites you to celebrate the beauty of love in all its forms.

Welcome to a tale where commitment knows no bounds, and love reigns supreme.

A Call To Action

Dear Readers,

As we share the pages of *A Royal Commitment: Ten Years of Marriage and Activism* with you, we invite you to join us in a call to action. This memoir is not just a recounting of our personal journey but a shared narrative that advocates for love, inclusivity, and positive change.

Here's how you can be a part of the movement:

1. **Spread the Message:** Share your thoughts and favorite excerpts from the memoir on social media. Use the hashtag #ARoyalCommitment to connect with others who resonate with the themes of love and activism.

2. **Engage in Conversations:** Initiate and participate in conversations about LGBTQIA+ rights, love, and inclusivity. Encourage open dialogue within your communities to foster understanding and acceptance.

3. **Support LGBTQIA+ Organizations:** Consider making a contribution or volunteering your time to organizations dedicated to promoting LGBTQIA+ rights and providing support to the community.

4. **Educate Yourself:** Stay informed about LGBTQIA+ history, challenges, and successes. Knowledge is a powerful tool in dismantling stereotypes and fostering empathy.

5. **Be an Ally:** Stand up against discrimination and prejudice. Be an ally to the LGBTQIA+ community by actively promoting inclusivity and acceptance in your personal and professional spheres.

6. **Celebrate Diversity:** Embrace and celebrate the diversity of love. Recognize that everyone's journey is unique, and every love story is valid.

7. **Share Your Story:** If you feel comfortable, share your own experiences or stories of love and acceptance. Your narrative may inspire others and contribute to creating a more compassionate world.

Together, let's make a commitment to love, understanding, and positive change. Thank you for being a part of this journey.

With gratitude,

HRH Prince Manvendra Singh Gohil and HH Prince DeAndre, Duke of Hanumanteshwar

PART 1

A ROYAL BEGINNING (2013–2015)

1
The Beginning of Our Journey (2013)

In the vast digital landscape of 2009, amidst the burgeoning social media platforms, Prince Manvendra and Duke DeAndre's paths converged on Tagged. It was there, in the digital realm, that their journey together began. For Manvendra, fresh off his appearance in the BBC documentary *Undercover Princes*, it was a time of seeking companionship, while DeAndre was deeply entrenched in the world of fashion, drawing inspiration for his work at Christian Dior in Seattle, Washington. Their initial connection on Tagged blossomed into a friendship that transcended physical distance, their conversations effortlessly weaving together shared interests, dreams, and aspirations.

In January 2011, they finally had the opportunity to meet face-to-face in Mumbai. However, their time together was fleeting, as Manvendra was called away to join Oprah Winfrey in Chicago for a taping of her show, abruptly interrupting their budding connection.

In 2012, fate wove its intricate threads of destiny, guiding Prince Manvendra and Duke DeAndre to pivotal moments that would forever alter the course of their lives. It began with a serene sunset at the beach in Mumbai, where the energy of love enveloped them, blessing them with an undeniable connection that transcended geographical boundaries and societal norms. As the warm hues of the setting sun painted the sky, amidst the gentle lapping of the waves, they found solace in each other's presence, laying the foundation for a love that would endure the test of time.

That same year, another significant moment unfolded at the home of Mr. Purshottam Walavalkar, Prince Manvendra's music teacher in Vile Parle. Accompanied by Duke DeAndre, they embarked on a harmonium music lesson, and DeAndre and Mr. Purshottam formed a fast and meaningful relationship based on shared values and a profound understanding of the energy of crystals, deities, and devotional music integral to Manvendra's training. After an afternoon filled with worthwhile interactions and spiritual resonance, they ventured to the beach, where the breathtaking sunset served as a serene backdrop to their burgeoning love story.

Prince Manvendra and Duke DeAndre's path as gay royal partners began in 2013, a momentous year when they made history as the first same-sex royal couple to marry in India. Their wedding day was more than just a ceremony; it was a testament to their commitment to each other and a celebration of love triumphing over adversity. Surrounded by loved ones, Manvendra and DeAndre honored their cultural traditions while challenging societal norms. They knew that their union would face resistance, but the two were determined to pave the way for acceptance and equality. Their marriage symbolized the wisdom of love transcending boundaries and embracing authenticity.

DeAndre, also known as HH Prince DeAndre, Duke of Hanumanteshwar, hails from the United States. His journey in the beauty-fashion industry, as the founder of H1927 LLC and Creative Director of Hanumanteshwar 1927tmR, has been a source of inspiration. His creativity and passion for fashion mirror our shared commitment to breaking down barriers and advocating for inclusivity.

Prince Manvendra's journey as an LGBTQIA+ rights advocate began long before he met DeAndre. In 2000, Manvendra founded the Lakshya Trust to support HIV-positive LGBTQIA+ individuals in India, a country where homosexuality was still criminalized.

Despite the risks, he chose to come out publicly in 2006, determined to use his platform to fight for equality. DeAndre, witnessing Manvendra's journey from afar, was inspired by Prince Manvendra's courage and dedication to the cause.

When they finally met, their connection was instant. They shared a mutual respect for each other's activism and a deep desire to make a difference in the world. Together, Manvendra and DeAndre stood side by side at rallies, delivered impassioned speeches on LGBTQIA+ rights, and marched in Pride parades across the globe. Their collaboration has been instrumental in shaping the discourse around LGBTQIA+ rights, garnering attention from global media outlets and documentaries like *Pieces of Us*. This award-winning documentary film focuses on the intimate and personal journeys of five gay, straight, and transgender LGBTQIA+ hate crime survivors whose lives intertwine through the brave choice to take their recovery public, inspiring the survivor in all of us.

As Manvendra and DeAndre disembarked the train in India for DeAndre's third visit in March 2013, a sense of familiarity and anticipation enveloped him. Accompanied by Prince Manvendra, DeAndre was graciously invited to immerse himself in the rich culture of Rajpipla, Manvendra's ancestral kingdom. The journey had commenced in Mumbai, where they were honored to meet Manvendra's father, the Maharaja of Rajpipla, who extended a heartfelt invitation to the royal palace.

Stepping into the opulent palace grounds, DeAndre couldn't help but marvel at its splendor, a testament to centuries of heritage and tradition. Amidst the grandeur, DeAndre confided in Manvendra's father, the Maharaja, expressing his profound affection for Manvendra and his dreams of a shared future. To their astonishment and joy, Prince Manvendra's great-great-uncle, Prince Sureshwar Singh Gohil of Rajpipla proposed that DeAndre marry Manvendra, sealing the moment with a ring imbued with the wisdom of love.

In adherence to timeless rituals, DeAndre underwent traditional preparation and ceremonies, symbolizing his commitment to the family's legacy. Embracing the title of Duke of Hanumanteshwar, bestowed upon him at a picturesque cottage on the estate, Duke DeAndre felt a deep connection to the storied history of the Rajpipla lineage. The Scottish-inspired architecture of the summer palace, reminiscent of Windsor Castle, served as a poignant backdrop to their union, echoing the enduring spirit of love and tradition.

The pinnacle of their journey unfolded on March 23rd, 2013, as Duke DeAndre was ceremoniously knighted by Manvendra's esteemed great-great-uncle, under the watchful gaze of the Maharaja. In this sacred moment, the wisdom of love permeated every aspect of their union, reinforcing the bond between them and the noble lineage they were now a part of.

As the time to bid farewell to India approached, DeAndre grappled with the bittersweet reality of departure. Despite Prince Sureshwar Singh Gohil of Rajpipla and his wife urging him to remain in Rajpipla, DeAndre knew that honoring his commitments in America was paramount. Promising to return in January 2014, DeAndre left with a heart filled with gratitude and anticipation for his future with Manvendra.

Their story unfolds amidst the bustling corridors of Seattle International Airport, back in June 2013. As an Indian-American duo, they were well aware of the complexities that lay ahead, yet their hearts remained steadfast in their commitment. With the intention of celebrating their union both in the United States and in India, they embarked on a voyage fueled by love and determination.

Their plans for a poignant hand-holding ceremony in Albany, Oregon, on July 3rd encountered an unexpected twist. Stranded on the roadside due to a car breakdown during their journey from Seattle, despair threatened to overshadow their joy. But just when uncertainty loomed large, a benevolent stranger emerged, a beacon of hope in their hour of need.

Guided by the wisdom of love, this stranger lent them a helping hand, fixing their car and offering solace in the form of ice cream, a gesture that restored their faith in humanity. Despite the delay, they arrived at their ceremony, hearts brimming with gratitude for the serendipitous intervention that paved their way.

The Beginning of Our Journey (2013)

Amidst the enchanting ceremony held at an ethereal estate in Washington on July 7th, surrounded by loved ones, they forged memories that would endure a lifetime. Commemorating all three of their wedding anniversaries each year—March 23rd in India, July 3rd and 7th in the United States—they find solace in the simplicity of celebrating their cherished July 7th anniversary.

Their honeymoon unfolded amidst the embrace of nature, at a tranquil retreat nestled within the coastal mountains. Beneath the starlit sky, they reveled in the warmth of a crackling fire and the magic of outdoor cinema, cherishing each moment shared in love and laughter.

Exploring the windswept beaches of Newport, Oregon hand in hand, they marveled at the beauty that surrounded them, finding solace in each other's presence. Yet, amidst the joy, poignant farewells marked their departure from the United States.

Prince Manvendra carried with him some sad news, waiting to share it with Duke DeAndre while at the beach in Newport: Mr. Purshottam Walavalkar had cancer and would not survive. They held hands and talked about him fondly, embracing the wisdom of love as they cherished memories of their time with him.

Navigating through a myriad of emotions, they embarked on a new chapter in January 2014, embracing the promise of a life intertwined in India. With unwavering resolve and boundless affection, they faced the challenges that lay ahead, fortified by the transformative power of love.

Nestled into the warmth of Professor Ramesh Gangoli's living room in Seattle, Prince Manvendra and Duke DeAndre found themselves enveloped by the essence of love and resilience. As two gay men navigating life's labyrinth, their journey bore witness to the enduring strength of love—a force that defied convention, societal norms, and familial expectations, emerging triumphant with each challenge.

Their visit to Professor Gangoli, a revered disciple of Prince Manvendra's cherished music teacher, Mr. Purshottam Walavalkar, transcended mere acquaintance. It was a communion of kindred spirits, united by a shared ardor for music and mathematics, and shared fond memories of Mr. Purshottam's visit to Professor Gangoli's home in Seattle.

Within the intimate sanctuary of Professor Gangoli's home, the melodious strains of Prince Manvendra's harmonium wove a tapestry of Indian classical music, painting the air with hues of soul-stirring melodies. This very home had also hosted great Indian classical musicians. In that moment of sublime bliss, they found solace—a poignant affirmation of the boundless beauty that graces our world when we open our hearts to its myriad wonders.

Yet, amidst the symphony of harmonies, an unyielding resolve lingered—a solemn vow to confront the trials ahead, to challenge prejudice, and to champion the rights of LGBTQIA+ individuals. As they bid farewell to Professor Gangoli and embarked on their homeward journey, they chose the humble embrace of public transportation over the trappings of royalty. It was a symbolic gesture—a testament to the truth that their identities were not defined by titles or wealth but by the profound love that united them.

As Prince Manvendra delves into the tapestry of his existence, he is enveloped by a deep sense of gratitude for the remarkable souls who have woven their threads into the fabric of his journey. Among them, none radiated with as much brilliance as Mr. Purshottam Walavalkar—a maestro of music and a cherished confidant, whose presence bestowed upon his path an abundance of wisdom and compassion.

Their serendipitous encounter unfolded within the sacred confines of musical mastery back in May 2000 as Prince Manvendra embarked on a transformative odyssey under Mr. Walavalkar's mentorship. What commenced as a simple student-teacher dynamic swiftly blossomed into a profound camaraderie, steeped in mutual reverence and admiration.

The apex of their shared voyage materialized in June 2000 when Mr. Walavalkar received a prestigious invitation to perform for royalty—a testament to his unparalleled skill and artistry. Eager to honor their bond, Prince Manvendra extended a heartfelt invitation for him to grace Rajvant Palace with his enchanting melodies for his birthday celebration later that year.

The Beginning of Our Journey (2013)

Upon his arrival, Mr. Walavalkar was captivated by the palace's regal splendor, his incredulity melting away as he discovered the truth of Prince Manvendra's royal lineage. Far from diluting their connection, this revelation deepened their bond, forging their friendship in the crucible of authenticity and shared experience.

Throughout the years, Mr. Walavalkar's steadfast support served as a guiding light during Prince Manvendra's most turbulent moments. From the courageous journey of self-acceptance to the trials of navigating life's ebbs and flows, his sage advice and unwavering acceptance were steadfast companions on the voyage of self-discovery.

As the sands of time shifted and Mr. Walavalkar's health declined, their bond only grew stronger, transcending mere mentorship to embody the purest form of kinship. His unyielding spirit and boundless zest for life inspired Prince Manvendra to embrace his truth with unwavering fortitude and conviction.

In the twilight of his earthly pilgrimage, Mr. Walavalkar welcomed Duke DeAndre into his fold with open arms, recognizing in him a kindred spirit and fellow seeker of truth. Their shared ardor for spirituality and reverence for the mysteries of existence forged an unbreakable bond—one that would withstand the tests of time and transcend the boundaries of mortality.

Though Mr. Walavalkar's physical form may have departed this realm on January 13th, 2014, his legacy of love and enlightenment continues to resonate in the hearts of all who were touched by his grace. As Prince Manvendra pays homage to his memory, he is reminded of the profound truth that love, in its infinite wisdom, serves as the guiding light that illuminates their path and sustains them through life's myriad of trials and triumphs.

2
United in Vows

In January 2014, Prince Manvendra and Duke DeAndre found themselves amidst the vibrant streets of Mumbai. For Duke DeAndre, it was a journey into the heart of Prince Manvendra's world, a chance to understand the intricacies of his responsibilities and the depth of his heritage. As they arrived at the Royal Establishment Hanumanteshwar, Duke DeAndre couldn't help but feel a sense of awe at the grandeur of the estate, now faded but still pulsating with history.

Despite the ruins that surrounded them, there was an undeniable charm to the place. It was here, among the crumbling walls and overgrown gardens, that Duke DeAndre felt a connection to something greater than himself—the legacy of the Gohil dynasty, steeped in tradition and honor. Spending days exploring the estate, Duke DeAndre found himself drawn to the untamed wilderness that had reclaimed much of the land. Among the ancient bamboo groves, he sought refuge from the chaos of the world outside, finding solace in the whispers of the wind and the rustle of leaves.

It was during one of these moments of quiet reflection that Duke DeAndre experienced a profound awakening. Beneath the canopy of a bamboo tree, he felt a sense of clarity wash over him as if the universe itself was speaking to him through the language of nature. Armed with this newfound insight into angel card reading and crystal energy healing, Duke DeAndre ventured into the bustling streets of Mumbai, navigating the labyrinthine corridors of the fashion and Bollywood industries. Among the glitz and glamor, he encountered a myriad of characters, each with their own story to tell.

One such encounter that left a lasting impression on Duke DeAndre was with Guruwarya Hazrat Abdulbhai Babaji—a sage-like figure whose kindness transcended language barriers. His wisdom resonated deeply with him, offering guidance and perspective in a world that often felt overwhelming. Duke DeAndre had taken guidance from Babaji on several occasions, using the wisdom of love and the knowledge beyond the veil of eyesight to find the correct answers.

Throughout his journey, Prince Manvendra remained a steadfast presence by Duke DeAndre's side. His unwavering support was a beacon of light in moments of darkness, reminding him of the strength that comes from love and partnership. As they navigated the complexities of their respective worlds, they did so with a shared sense of purpose and commitment. Together, they faced challenges head-on, drawing strength from each other and the deep bond that held them together.

In the end, their journey was not just about discovering themselves; it was about forging a path forward guided by the wisdom of love. And as they looked to the future, they did so with hearts full of hope and a shared determination to make a difference in the world.

As Prince Manvendra and Duke DeAndre fondly reminisce about their inaugural royal tour, they reflect on its profound significance. Scheduled by the establishments, this tour is a customary tradition for newly married couples, aimed at visiting other kingdoms of importance to strengthen historic ties and announce the next generation of leadership.

Their journey to Cambay went beyond being a mere visit; it symbolized a reunion between two kingdoms deeply entrenched in centuries of intertwined history. Dating back approximately three hundred years, the Rajpipla royals generously provided sanctuary to an East African Sidi tribe, granting them refuge and the right to mine agate stones in the region of Ratanpur. These precious stones, mined with care and reverence, were then sent to the kingdom of Cambay for expert polishing.

Welcomed graciously by HH Nawab Mirza Mohammed Jafar Ali Khan Najam-es-sani and HH Begum Parvin Sultan Najam-es-sani Sahiba, their journey unfolded amidst a sense of reverence for the shared heritage that binds their families together. Amidst the opulence of a formal lunch at the palace, they found themselves immersed in the echoes of history, surrounded by artifacts and tales of a bygone era.

However, their visit wasn't without its challenges. In a moment of peril during the lunch, Duke DeAndre found himself in a harrowing situation when a chicken bone became lodged in his throat. The swift action of the royal attendants averted disaster, but the incident served as a stark reminder of life's unpredictability and the fragility of their mortal existence.

Undeterred by the close call, they ventured forth into the afternoon, eager to explore the treasures and mysteries that Cambay had to offer. From the gleaming workshops of jewelers to the ancient cliffside palaces and sacred shrines, each moment was infused with a sense of awe and wonder, heightened by the knowledge of their shared ancestral ties.

Intrigued by whispers of a looming curse rumored to haunt the palace, Duke DeAndre felt compelled to investigate further, much to Prince Manvendra's apprehension. Together, they delved into the labyrinthine corridors of the palace, drawn by the allure of hidden secrets and ancient mysteries.

Yet, their quest for answers took an unexpected turn when Duke DeAndre was overcome by a momentary loss of consciousness, sending shock waves of fear through their entourage. In a testament to Prince Manvendra's unwavering resolve, he sprang into action, rallying the royal attendants to his aid.

Amidst the chaos, their spirits remained unbroken, buoyed by the support and camaraderie of those around them. Though their time in Cambay was brief, it left an indelible mark on their hearts, serving as a poignant reminder of the enduring bonds of kinship and the timeless power of shared history.

Meanwhile, Prince Manvendra received a message from his father, the Maharaja of Rajpipla, summoning them back to the king's palace in Rajpipla upon their return from Cambay. As they bid farewell to Cambay and returned to the embrace of the king's palace, they carried with them not only memories of adventure and danger but also invaluable lessons learned. The guidance and kindness shown to them by the Begum of Cambay served as a beacon of light, illuminating the path ahead as they navigated the complexities of royal life together.

As Duke DeAndre and Prince Manvendra reflect on a pivotal moment that tested the strength of their bond, their hearts brim with gratitude and mutual admiration. Their marriage, forged across different cultural backgrounds, stands as a beacon of the enduring power of true love and connections that defy societal norms.

The incident in question arose when the establishment orchestrated a scheme against Duke DeAndre, aiming to detain him for the seemingly innocuous act of accompanying Prince Manvendra to the local market. Such actions were deemed inappropriate for his title of Duke, reflecting the rigid enforcement of societal hierarchy within their realm.

Upon uncovering the sinister plot, Prince Manvendra's father, the Maharaja of Rajpipla, intervened, alerting him to the imminent danger facing Duke DeAndre. Distressed by the gravity of the situation, Prince Manvendra wasted no time in conveying the urgent message to his dear husband, urging him to exercise caution.

Despite the looming threat, they resolved to maintain their course, refusing to cower in the face of intimidation. Duke DeAndre swiftly and discreetly packed his belongings, and under the cloak of darkness, a waiting car spirited him away to the safety of Mumbai, beyond the clutches of harm.

Reflecting on the harrowing ordeal, they are deeply appreciative of the timely warning and decisive action that enabled Duke DeAndre's escape. It served as a stark reminder that even within the corridors of royalty, danger can lurk, but with unwavering support and trusted allies, they emerged unscathed.

For Duke DeAndre, the experience was a poignant testament to the significance of Prince Manvendra's steadfast support and guidance. It underscored the importance of exercising caution in navigating the treacherous waters of establishment hostility, a lesson he embraced with humility and gratitude.

In the end, Prince Manvendra's father's vigilant warning proved invaluable, as Duke DeAndre skillfully evaded the clutches of the establishment. Their enduring marriage emerged unscathed, serving as a profound reminder that genuine connections transcend the confines of societal conventions.

Their shared experience, steeped in the wisdom of love, reaffirmed their belief in the transformative power of kindness and compassion, triumphing over the forces of hate and bigotry. As proud husbands, they stand united, committed to inspiring others to embrace solidarity and extend unconditional support to all.

As Prince Manvendra reflects on the intricate tapestry of his life's journey, one moment stands out like a shimmering gem: his appearance on Oprah Winfrey's iconic show, *Where Are They Now?* It was his third encounter with the luminous screens of the Oprah Winfrey Network (OWN), yet this time, the format diverged from the usual studio sit-down. Instead, the production team chose to capture glimpses of his life in motion, a decision that would profoundly shape the narrative of his advocacy.

In 2014, during his tour in Michigan, Prince Manvendra made a pivotal decision—to launch the Free Gay India campaign on August 15th, coinciding with India's Independence Day. The announcement of this campaign marked a significant turning point in his advocacy efforts. During the campaign launch, he proudly declared the involvement of the LGBTQIA+ community and their allies in the international advocacy for LGBTQIA+ rights in India.

Back to his appearance on Oprah's show, he seized the opportunity to inform her of his upcoming trip to Michigan, where he was scheduled to inaugurate the Kirby, a hotel project spearheaded by his close friend, Chicago-based lawyer Jay Paul Deratany. Oprah herself took an interest in the endeavor, dispatching her team to document his interviews within the hotel's walls and capture the meticulous preparations leading up to the grand inauguration.

During the interview, Prince Manvendra opened up to Oprah, baring the intricacies of his personal journey. He spoke of the profound reconciliation within his family and the generous gift bestowed upon him by his father—the royal establishment of Hanumanteshwar. With unwavering candor, he shared the harsh realities faced by the LGBTQIA+ community in India, particularly in light of the reimplementation of Section 377 of the Indian Penal Code, which unjustly criminalizes same-sex relationships.

His appearance on Oprah's esteemed platform was more than just a televised moment; it was a clarion call for change, a plea for justice, and a testament to the resilience of the human spirit. It served as a potent catalyst to amplify his narrative and shed light on the formidable challenges confronting the LGBTQIA+ community in India. And amidst it all, the guiding force of love remained steadfast, anchoring him firmly to his path of advocacy and enlightenment.

Prince Manvendra and Duke DeAndre have encountered a myriad of hurdles along the winding path of their journey together. One such obstacle presented itself in July 2014, when Duke DeAndre found himself compelled to depart from India due to restrictive visa regulations imposed by the Indian government, which refused to recognize marriage equality. This necessitated a temporary sojourn outside the country before he could return.

Embracing the silver lining of this predicament, Duke DeAndre seized the opportunity to explore the enchanting land of Nepal—a country steeped in rich history and breathtaking natural beauty. His itinerary was brimming with plans to finalize a book project, savor delectable culinary delights, and indulge in the vibrant shopping scene that Kathmandu had to offer.

Opting to reside in Thamel, Kathmandu's bustling epicenter of commerce and cuisine, brought him in close proximity to the hallowed grounds of the royal palace, despite the somber echoes of tragedy that resonated within its walls. Yet, amidst the tapestry of

Kathmandu's bustling streets, he found solace and companionship in the warmth of a local jeweler family, whose humble shop became a sanctuary of sorts during his stay.

In the tranquil embrace of their establishment, he whiled away leisurely hours, forging genuine connections and relishing in the shared camaraderie. It was there that he embarked on a captivating journey of collaboration, commissioning a breathtaking jewelry suite adorned with Himalayan diamonds, emeralds, and pearls—a tangible testament to the bonds forged and memories created during his time in Nepal.

As the time came to bid farewell to the picturesque landscapes and newfound friendships of Nepal, his heart swelled with a bittersweet blend of nostalgia and anticipation. Yet, amidst the poignant farewells, Prince Manvendra and Duke DeAndre found themselves steeped in a profound sense of gratitude for the transformative power of travel and exploration.

For them, each obstacle encountered along their journey serves as a poignant reminder of the resilience and strength that defines their bond. Despite the hurdles and hardships, they stand united in their unwavering resolve to embrace life's adventures with open arms, fortified by the enduring friendships woven into the fabric of their shared narrative. As they chart their course forward, hand in hand, they eagerly anticipate the myriad of adventures that await them, guided by the wisdom gleaned from their collective experiences and the boundless love that illuminates their path.

3
Navigating Royal Realities

As Prince Manvendra and Duke DeAndre embarked on their journey to attend the wedding of Prince Shivendra Singh Bhati of Jaisalmer, anticipation filled the air. The venue, Mandir Palace, held a special place in their hearts, as it was where Prince Manvendra's mother, the Queen of Rajpipla, had spent her formative years. Their road trip from Rajpipla, Gujarat, to Jaisalmer promised hours on National Highway 48, winding through the captivating desert landscape.

Just as they reached Jaisalmer, ready to partake in the festivities, Prince Manvendra's phone rang. It was Princess Krishna Kumari of Rajpipla, his aunt, bearing sad news. She informed them that Prince Manvendra's grandmother, HH Rani Jayendra Kumari of Rajpipla, had been diagnosed with stomach cancer. The news cast a somber shadow over their excitement for the upcoming celebrations.

As they traversed the desert terrain en route to Jaisalmer, the sun's golden rays painted the sands in a mesmerizing hue. Yet, their journey hit a snag when a sudden jolt and the sound of a shredded tire brought them to an abrupt halt, leaving them stranded in the vast desert expanse. Panic threatened to engulf them as they realized they had no spare tire to replace the damaged one.

Just when despair seemed to take hold, a group of strangers on motorbikes appeared on the horizon, like a ray of hope in their moment of need. Their kindness knew no bounds as they swiftly came to their aid, providing a spare tire from a nearby village and ensuring the safety of their vehicle. Their selflessness left them deeply humbled and immensely grateful.

With the tire replaced, they resumed their journey to Jaisalmer, where the excitement of the impending wedding awaited them. Attending this grand occasion, graced by members of esteemed royal families, held immense significance for them—it was a historic moment where the crown family of Rajpipla and Duke DeAndre stood together.

The wedding ceremony, held in February 2015, unfolded against the majestic backdrop of Mandir Palace, adorned with cascading floral arrangements and twinkling lights. Amidst the age-old customs and rituals, they witnessed the profound love shared between the bride and groom, their joy palpable in the air.

Following the ceremony, a sumptuous feast awaited them, showcasing the rich flavors of Rajasthani cuisine. Surrounded by the laughter and camaraderie of esteemed guests, they reveled in the joyous atmosphere, feeling privileged to be part of such a momentous occasion.

As the night wore on, the air resonated with the melodies of traditional music, and the dance floor came alive with spirited celebrations. Amidst the jubilant throng of family members, they danced with abandon, swept up in the infectious energy of the moment.

The wedding of Prince Shivendra Singh Bhati of Jaisalmer served as a poignant reminder of the enduring power of love, tradition, and unity. For Prince Manvendra and Duke DeAndre, it was a cherished experience—one that they will forever hold close to their hearts, grateful for the opportunity to share in its splendor and significance.

As Prince Manvendra reflects on the chilling incident that unfolded during his husband, Duke DeAndre's, visit to the Royal Establishment Hanumanteshwar, he is flooded with gratitude that Duke DeAndre emerged unscathed from the ordeal. As partners in life and advocates for change, Prince Manvendra and Duke DeAndre understand all too well the risks that come with being public figures championing controversial causes. Duke DeAndre's trip to the royal establishment was meant to oversee the development of the LGBTQIA+ community campus and sustainable initiatives. However, what should have been a routine visit turned into a nightmare when he fell victim to poisoning during a meal, orchestrated by a member of the staff.

Prince Manvendra comes from a family where royal conspiracies have not been uncommon, but it was a firsthand experience for him to encounter a poisoning strategy enforced on his husband, Duke DeAndre. They had just been living together in India for two years. He felt the need to be more aware of the dangers existing around them, and that they both need to be cautious of the people surrounding them. Though Duke DeAndre was able to recover from the poisoning, Prince Manvendra learned a lesson that it's difficult to trust in the royal establishment.

The poisoning, a blatant attempt to derail their efforts to create a safe space for the LGBTQIA+ community, served as a stark reminder of the dangers activists face in their pursuit of social justice. Yet, amidst the darkness, they found strength in the unwavering power of love. With swift medical intervention, Duke DeAndre made a full recovery, his resilience serving as a beacon of hope in the face of adversity.

As advocates for LGBTQIA+ rights and members of the Indian nobility, Prince Manvendra and Duke DeAndre understand the gravity of their responsibility in standing up for marginalized communities and fighting for social justice. This incident only strengthened their resolve to amplify the voices of the oppressed and push for tangible change.

For them, this was not just an external issue—it struck at the core of their personal beliefs and experiences. It reminded them of the discrimination and violence that LGBTQIA+ individuals face daily. Despite the risks, their commitment to this cause remains unwavering. The path to social justice may be fraught with obstacles, but it's a journey they're determined to undertake together.

In Duke DeAndre, Prince Manvendra sees not only a loving partner but also a fearless ally in the battle for equality. Together, they stand firm in their quest for a fairer and more inclusive world for all LGBTQIA+ individuals. Though the road ahead may be challenging, their bond and shared dedication to social justice give them strength. As they continue their advocacy work, they take solace in the enduring wisdom of love, knowing that their collective efforts will pave the way for a brighter tomorrow.

February 8th, 2015, remains etched in Prince Manvendra's memory as a solemn day, marked by the departure of his grandmother, the esteemed HH Rani Jayendra Kumari of Rajpipla. The news of her passing struck him deeply, evoking a flood of memories and emotions. Fresh from attending a wedding in Baroda, Prince Manvendra and his husband embarked on the journey to Mumbai to pay their respects.

As they journeyed, their hearts heavy with the loss, they took on the somber task of informing relatives and friends of Granny's departure. Despite their efforts, they arrived too late for her cremation procession. However, they managed to reach her funeral pyre just in time to bid her a final farewell.

In the days that followed, Prince Manvendra remained steadfast in his commitment to honoring Granny's memory, diligently fulfilling the rituals outlined in her will under the guidance of her brother, the King of Lakhtar. It was a time of deep introspection, where he found himself contemplating Granny's enduring legacy and the profound impact she had on their lives through the wisdom of love.

Prince Manvendra was the favorite and most pampered grandson of his grandmother, her late Highness Rani Jayendra Kumari of Rajpipla. His Granny had been a trained violinist in her childhood in the royal family of Lakhtar, and she always encouraged Prince Manvendra to pursue his talent in playing the harmonium since she felt that the prince had a gift from God in Indian classical music. So much so that before she died, she gifted him her personal violin she used to play in the 1940s. Prince Manvendra took her on some adventurous pilgrimages in India. Once, they both rode on horseback for almost eight hours to see the beginning of the holy river Ganges where the glacier melted into a river. Despite the risk involved, he ensured that Granny was brought back safely and fulfilled his spiritual obligation as the grandson.

Prince Manvendra shared a special bond with Granny, one that was particularly poignant during his last visit to her in the hospital. As she held his hand, a sense of peace emanated from her, and she whispered, "Son, now I can depart in tranquility knowing you're cared for." Her affection for his husband, Duke DeAndre, was unmistakable, and her unwavering support for their union resonated deeply with them both.

Despite the controversies their relationship stirred within certain circles, Granny's unwavering belief in the power of love underscored the possibility of progress and acceptance, even in the face of adversity. Her passing left a void in their family, yet it also served to bring them closer together, reinforcing the importance of cherishing their loved ones and honoring their legacies.

Granny's remarkable life and unwavering resilience continue to inspire them, serving as a guiding light for generations to come. They hold her memory close to their hearts and strive each day to embody the values she held dear, embracing the wisdom of love and the strength it imparts to them all.

In April 2015, Prince Manvendra and Duke DeAndre's journey took a meaningful turn as they found themselves collaborating with organizations devoted to the betterment of the LGBTQIA+ community. Among these impactful alliances was the AIDS Healthcare Foundation (AHF), a global leader headquartered in Los Angeles, dedicated to HIV testing and treatment.

Their involvement with AHF traces back to 2013 when Prince Manvendra initiated Impulse Group, a chapter focused on LGBTQIA+ sexual health in India. It was a deeply fulfilling endeavor, guided by the wisdom of love and their unwavering dedication to the cause.

In 2015, during her visit to Mumbai, Ms. Terri Ford, AHF's Chief of Global Advocacy and Policy, honored Prince Manvendra by appointing him as AHF's Brand Ambassador for India. This appointment was a historic moment, underscoring AHF's recognition of his advocacy efforts and reflecting the wisdom of love in their decision.

Since then, Prince Manvendra's journey with AHF has taken him to Los Angeles, where he has forged partnerships and received accolades on behalf of the organization. In 2018, both Prince Manvendra and Duke DeAndre were present at the inauguration of AHF India Cares Centre of Excellence in Delhi, showcasing their shared commitment to the cause.

Their bond with AHF extends beyond professional collaboration. They were honored to attend the wedding of AHF's Terri Ford and her spouse, Trish Moran, in Newport, California, celebrating their love and support for each other. Prince Manvendra and Duke DeAndre were touched by the warm hospitality rendered by Trish and Terri when they both personally came to greet them at the LA airport and drove them to the hotel where arrangements were made for the wedding guests to stay. The wedding was on a yacht, which was specially docked for the prince and the duke so that they could go to the airport to fly to San Francisco to be part of pride celebrations. Trish and Terri also flew into New York to participate in the fundraising event hosted for the prince and duke as part of the World Pride celebrations in 2019.

The following year, Prince Manvendra's connection with AHF deepened when he was invited to present awards at an event hosted by the Gay Men's Chorus in Los Angeles. His impassioned speech caught the attention of AHF's president, leading to a significant lunch meeting where they delved into the pressing issues faced by the LGBTQIA+ community in India.

As they continue their journey towards inclusivity and acceptance for the LGBTQIA+ community, Prince Manvendra and Duke DeAndre remain deeply grateful for AHF's unwavering support and partnership. Their tireless dedication to HIV testing and treatment reflects the wisdom of love, inspiring them to work towards creating a better future for all.

Gathered in the Durbar Hall at Rajvant Palace, the heart of the royal family of Rajpipla, a profound sense of pride and joy enveloped Prince Manvendra and Duke DeAndre. It was October 2015, and they were celebrating a two-day music festival in honor of Prince Manvendra's fiftieth birthday. They were deeply moved to see their loved ones and esteemed guests from around the world come together. For years, Prince Manvendra had marked his birthday with an Indian classical music event, providing a platform for young artists nationwide to showcase their talents in vocal music, instrumental music, and dance forms. They always invited renowned musicians, nurturing emerging talent and offering them valuable exposure.

This year held a special significance, not only because it was Prince Manvendra's milestone fiftieth birthday but also because it symbolized the journey they had undertaken as a couple in a society that had long resisted change. As members of the Rajpipla royal family, they understood the challenges of openly acknowledging their relationship. Yet, they were resolute in leveraging their platform to advocate for acceptance and empathy. Surrounded by the grandeur of the Durbar Hall, they were embraced by familiar faces, from Manvendra's father to cousins, extended family, and international royals.

Their joy was amplified by the presence of foreign guests who had traveled from the United States to share in their special occasion. As the melodies of the music filled the hall and the dancers gracefully moved, they felt a profound connection to their culture and heritage. As proud members of the Rajpipla royal family, they also took pride in being gay men who utilized their status to advocate for acceptance and understanding.

As members of the royal family, Prince Manvendra and Duke DeAndre have graced numerous social gatherings, yet none quite compare to the ones hosted by their friends, the sisters Mimi and Shameem.

Their acquaintance with Mimi dates back to 2007 when Prince Manvendra first met her in Mumbai at the memorial service of their mutual friend, Janet Fine. Over time, they formed a close bond, often socializing together at country clubs, Mimi's residence, or the D. M. Botawala orphanage for the girls. Following Duke DeAndre's relocation to India in 2014, Prince Manvendra introduced him to Mimi during a talk at a women's club in Mumbai, where Duke DeAndre showcased his talents in angel card readings and the use of crystals. Mimi's open-mindedness led to her enjoyment of Duke DeAndre's spiritual guidance sessions.

Among the array of social events, one occasion stands out—the winter party hosted by the D. M. Girls Orphanage Trust, under the leadership of Sheila E. U. Botawala, Mimi and Shameem's mother. The warmth of Sheila's affection and the festive ambiance forge a deep connection, especially when Duke DeAndre plays the role of Santa Claus, delighting the girls with gifts and spreading cheer. The gathering, attended by friends and diplomats, and adorned with vibrant performances by the children, becomes a treasured memory.

The party is not just about entertainment; it's about fostering genuine connections amidst the laughter and celebration. Mimi's piano skills grace the evening with elegance, infusing her Mumbai home with a captivating charm that sets the stage for camaraderie among diplomats, artists, and industrialists.

Beyond her musical prowess, Mimi's literary work, *Insight*, delves into the intricacies of human experience, while Shameem manages the D. M. Girls Orphanage Trust, providing essential shelter and education for girls. Their dedication resonates deeply with Prince Manvendra and Duke DeAndre, underscoring the transformative power of education in shaping futures and nurturing communities.

As allies of the LGBTQIA+ community, Prince Manvendra and Duke DeAndre recognize the significance of creating inclusive spaces where individuals can embrace their identities. Mimi and Shameem's gatherings epitomize universal values of love and acceptance, bridging societal divides and fostering understanding.

Driven by a commitment to advocate for causes close to their hearts, whether it's arts, education, or LGBTQIA+ rights, Prince Manvendra and Duke DeAndre find inspiration in Mimi and Shameem's events. These occasions exemplify the profound impact of compassion and cultural appreciation, motivating them to continue effecting positive change in the world.

In honoring Sheila E. U. Botawala's legacy, they stand united with Mimi and Shameem in their dedication to the D. M. Girls Orphanage Trust, recognizing education as the catalyst for change.

Through their collective efforts, they sow the seeds for a brighter future.

Mimi and Shameem's gatherings serve as emblems of kindness and cultural celebration, reminding Prince Manvendra and Duke DeAndre of the beauty in diversity and the strength found in unity. They cherish the friendship shared with Mimi and Shameem, acknowledging the profound influence these relationships have had on their lives. With love and understanding, they strive to create a more inclusive and compassionate world for all.

"Captured at sunset on the beach in 2012, this moment marks when Prince Manvendra and DeAndre first felt the profound wisdom of love energies."

The Summer Palace of the Royal Establishment Hanumanteshwar, built in 1925 and styled after a Scottish castle, elegantly stands beside the Narmada River.

"Prince Manvendra and DeAndre enjoying a music concert in Mumbai, 2012."

Prince Manvendra stands beside this broken-down car on Interstate 5, where a kind stranger stopped to help them on the journey to Albany, OR for the Handfasting Ceremony.

Prince Manvendra and Duke DeAndre celebrate with friends and family in Albany, OR, following their beautiful Handfasting Ceremony.

Prince Manvendra and Duke DeAndre's wedding at the Enchanted Estate in Washington State, July 2013. Duke DeAndre is wearing red, the color of Mars, which – according to Hindu astrology – is the planet that oversees marriage, while Prince Manvendra is adorned in green, symbolizing life, rebirth, fertility, harmony, and freshness.

"Left to right: Duke DeAndre, Prince Manvendra, Rani Tara Devi Gohil (great aunt), Maharaja Raghubir Singh Gohil (Manvendra's father, the king), Maharaj Sureshwar Singh Gohil (great uncle who knighted DeAndre as Duke)."

"Prince Manvendra and Duke DeAndre greeting guests at the King's Palace in Rajpipla during the music festival celebrating Prince Manvendra's birthday, 2014."

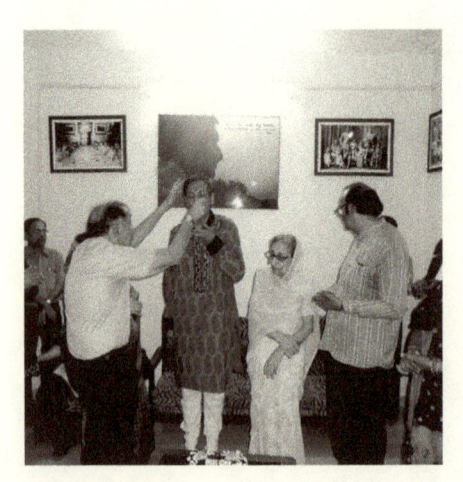

"Celebration at Hanumanteshwar for the wedding anniversary of the Prince and Duke. The oldest members of the Rajpipla Royal family giving honor: Rani Jayendra Kumari (Granny) stands to the right of Prince Manvendra, Maharaj Sureshwar Singh Gohil feeds Prince Manvendra cake, with Maharaja Raghubir Singh Gohil presiding over the festivities."

"Gems purchased by Duke DeAndre in Kathmandu, Nepal during his first trip in 2014."

"Duke DeAndre modeling the new jewelry collection along with traditional men's fashion designed by a Bollywood fashion designer. Location: Malad West home, Mumbai, 2014."

"Prince Manvendra and Duke DeAndre enjoying an evening at Rajvant Palace, also known as the King's Palace, located in Rajpipla, Gujarat, India."

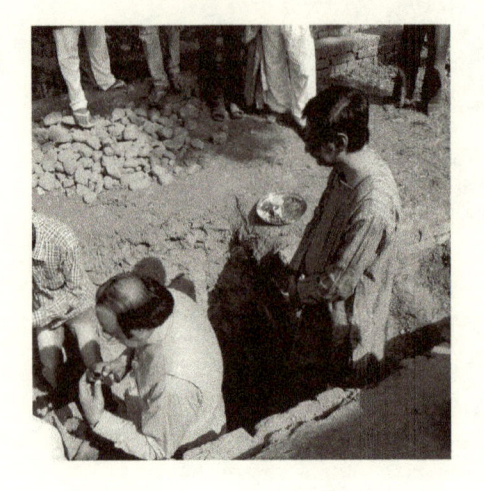

"Maharaja Raghubir Singh Gohil laying the artifacts during the foundation stone laying ceremony for the LGBTQIA+ community campus ashram in Rajpipla. The symbolic foundation stone marks the site for a new building, with Prince Manvendra at the Royal Establishment of Hanumanteshwar."

"The Hitesh Barot Library and Learning Center, gifted by Surendra Barot in memory of Hitesh Barot, who tragically died from a crocodile attack while swimming in the Narmada River."

"Duke DeAndre, the architect behind the design of the LGBTQIA+ community campus and the extension of Janet Cottage, initially drew up the plan on a napkin during a road trip from Mumbai to Rajpipla."

PART 2

THE INTERSECTION OF LOVE AND ADVOCACY (2016-2018)

4
Voices Unveiled

As they reminisce about their time at the Royal Establishment Hanumanteshwar, one memory stands out vividly—the presence of their beloved Carmel. This caramel-colored Indian street dog found solace near the front gate of their estate, adopting it as his home. Each morning, Duke DeAndre would place a bowl of food and water near the bushes where Carmel would emerge slowly to nourish himself. Carmel had carved out a space in the earth where he sought refuge and rest. Amidst the other dogs on the estate, Carmel held a special place in their hearts, particularly Duke DeAndre's, as he affectionately named him Carmel.

However, one morning, their hearts sank as they discovered Carmel's back leg injured, likely caught in a trap or harmed by someone perturbed by animals near their crops. Swiftly, Duke DeAndre sought aid from Prince Manvendra, knowing of his family's connection to a veterinary hospital established by them in the 1920s. Despite initial hesitations from the veterinarians, they persisted in their efforts. Determined to help Carmel, Duke DeAndre ventured into the bushes to retrieve him, enduring a bite during the rescue that led him to seek medical attention for rabies shots.

Despite their best efforts, Carmel's condition failed to improve. Duke DeAndre turned to social media for help, leading to the intervention of VCARE, Vadodara Centre for Animal Rescue and Emergency. Together, Prince Manvendra and Duke DeAndre transported Carmel to the hospital, where he received the necessary care and rehabilitation for three months before returning to Hanumanteshwar.

Yet, their happiness was short-lived. On the night of Prince Manvendra's birthday celebration at the King's Palace, Duke DeAndre discovered Carmel missing. Despite their efforts to search the vast fifteen-acre estate, overgrown with vegetation, Carmel remained elusive. Tragically, wildlife officials later informed them that Carmel had fallen prey to a leopard, his life abruptly cut short.

The loss of Carmel deeply impacted them; he had become an integral part of their family, and his absence left a void in their hearts. Nevertheless, his memory remains etched within them, a testament to the bond they shared and the love they showered upon him. Though he may no longer roam the grounds of Hanumanteshwar, his spirit lives on, immortalized in their cherished memories and the pages of their book.

Visiting Lakhtar Fort City and meeting HRH Thakur Balbhadra Singh held profound significance for Prince Manvendra and Duke DeAndre, especially considering the recent passing of his sister, her late Highness Rani Jayendra Kumari of Rajpipla. Their familial bond added depth to their visit, resonating with the shared history and legacy between their families.

Welcomed warmly by HRH Thakur Balbhadra Singh, they embarked on a journey through the rich tapestry of Lakhtar's history. The fort city, despite its aging facade, exuded an air of timeless grandeur, echoing the stories of generations past. Each step they took unveiled new wonders and hidden treasures, each imbued with the spirit of their ancestral lineage.

From the ancient stepwell to the meticulously preserved royal family temple, every corner of Lakhtar Fort City spoke volumes about the pride and reverence the siblings held for their heritage. As they navigated the labyrinthine corridors, they were enveloped in the echoes of history, feeling a deep connection to the resilience and fortitude of their lineage. Yet, it was not just the physical splendor of Lakhtar that left a lasting impression on them. It was the warmth and hospitality of HRH Thakur Balbhadra Singh and her late Highness Rani Jayendra Kumari that touched their hearts. Their bond as siblings was palpable, infusing their visit with a sense of familial warmth and camaraderie.

Both Duke DeAndre and Prince Manvendra were touched by the warm royal hospitality extended by HRH Thakur Balbhadra Singh of Lakhtar when he served one of the tastiest vegetarian foods offered to Duke DeAndre. He ensured that the food was cooked without red and green chilies, which Duke DeAndre was allergic to, and also gave them buttermilk made from their own cows' milk. He also entertained Duke DeAndre by telling him stories of his childhood spent with his sister, her late Highness Rani Jayendra Kumari of Rajpipla, Prince Manvendra's grandmother.

As they reflected on their journey through Lakhtar, their thoughts turned to the LGBTQIA+ community in India. Despite the progress made, challenges remain. However, the unwavering support of figures like HRH Thakur Balbhadra Singh and her late Highness Rani Jayendra Kumari instills hope for a more inclusive future.

Their visit to Lakhtar Fort City served as a poignant reminder of the enduring values of love and acceptance that define Indian society at its best. It strengthened their resolve to advocate for LGBTQIA+ rights and work towards a more inclusive society.

Leaving Lakhtar, they carried with them not only memories of its rich history but also a renewed sense of purpose and determination. They are deeply thankful for the hospitality shown to them by HRH Thakur Balbhadra Singh and for the enduring spirit of inclusivity that characterizes the cultural fabric of India.

Joy Rahut, a close friend of Prince Manvendra, had been a royal guest at Rajpipla's palace long before Prince Manvendra's marriage to Duke DeAndre. During that visit, he extended an invitation to Prince Manvendra to visit his tea estate in Kailashpur. After their marriage, Prince Manvendra introduced Joy to Duke DeAndre, and despite Joy's eccentric nature, both Prince Manvendra and Duke DeAndre decided to honor the long-standing invitation.

In 2016, Prince Manvendra and Duke DeAndre embarked on a remarkable journey to the Kailashpur tea estate. Nestled at the foothills of the Himalayas in the Western Dooars region, the estate offered unparalleled beauty and rich heritage. This visit held profound significance for them, providing a glimpse into the intricate world of tea production and the enduring legacy of Joy Rahut's family, who had stewarded the estate for generations.

Upon their arrival, they were warmly greeted by Joy Rahut, who graciously shared the estate's illustrious history. It was awe-inspiring to learn about the Rahut family's unwavering commitment to producing some of the world's finest teas for over a century. As they embarked on a tour of the estate, they were captivated by the lush surroundings, teeming with diverse wildlife, and the majestic Himalayan peaks casting their enchanting spell in the distance.

Their exploration led them to the heart of the tea factory, where they witnessed the meticulous process of tea manufacturing firsthand. The dedication and precision evident in every step underscored the Rahut family's commitment to excellence. Sampling the freshly brewed tea was a sensory delight, evoking a profound appreciation for the craftsmanship and artistry involved in producing such exquisite blends.

Beyond the tea estate's remarkable offerings, they were deeply moved by the story of its origins. Learning about the resilience and determination of the Rahut family, who overcame numerous challenges to establish the Kailashpur plantation, filled them with admiration. The estate's accolades and recognition by the Tea Board further underscored its exceptional quality and contribution to the industry.

In Hindu mythology, the name "Kailash" carries profound symbolism, evoking images of divine beauty and spiritual serenity. Indeed, their visit to the estate transported them to a realm of enchantment, where the harmonious blend of nature's bounty and human ingenuity cast a spell of timeless allure.

As they immersed themselves in the tranquil ambiance of the estate, they couldn't help but reflect on the profound connection between nature, heritage, and human endeavor. They are deeply grateful to Joy Rahut and his family for graciously sharing their legacy with them. Kailashpur's enduring legacy and unparalleled beauty serve as a poignant reminder of the transformative power of love, dedication, and perseverance.

As Prince Manvendra and Duke DeAndre, they've weathered their share of storms, but one moment in 2016 serves as a stark reminder of the fragility of security in the face of adversity. It was the eve of the Los Angeles Pride Parade, an event they had eagerly anticipated, only to be jolted by the news of the tragic mass shooting at the Pulse nightclub in Orlando, Florida.

The weight of the tragedy hung heavy in the air, casting a somber shadow over the festivities. The loss of forty-nine innocent lives and the injuries sustained by fifty-three others reverberated across the nation, leaving them and countless others reeling in shock and disbelief. Suddenly, the joyous celebration of love and pride was overshadowed by fear and uncertainty.

As news of the shooting spread, concerns about the safety of public gatherings like the Los Angeles Pride Parade surged. In response, the Los Angeles Police Department (LAPD) sprang into action, implementing stringent security measures to safeguard participants and spectators alike. Their swift and decisive response was a testament to their unwavering commitment to public safety.

On the morning of the parade, tensions were palpable as security forces remained on high alert. Reports of an individual apprehended near the parade route with firearms only heightened anxiety levels, prompting thorough investigations and additional security precautions. Despite the apprehension, Prince Manvendra and Duke DeAndre were reassured by the presence of their personal security details, provided to ensure their safety throughout the event.

As they rode in a red Mustang convertible driven by Terri Ford and Trish Moran as part of the LA AHF Pride contingency, Prince Manvendra and Duke DeAndre felt the streets pulsating with energy and resilience. Yet, amidst the uncertainty, there was also a profound sense of solidarity—a shared determination to stand tall in the face of adversity and reclaim their right to love and live freely.

The LAPD's meticulous security measures proved effective as the parade unfolded without incident, drawing tens of thousands of spirited participants and supporters. Their unwavering vigilance and dedication ensured that the parade remained a beacon of hope and resilience in the wake of tragedy.

Looking back, they are deeply grateful for the LAPD's steadfast commitment to their safety and the safety of all who attended the parade. Their actions underscored the crucial role that authorities play in preserving peace and security, particularly in times of crisis. As advocates for LGBTQIA+ rights, they remain steadfast in their pursuit of a future where love can flourish without fear, and where every individual can embrace their true self without reservation.

5
Love in the Spotlight

In 2017, Duke DeAndre and Prince Manvendra embarked on a deeply personal and transformative journey as they proudly unveiled their private fashion label, H1927. Rooted in the Royal Establishment of Hanumanteshwar, the Rajpipla summer palace's front gate, built in 1927, two years after the Scottish-inspired castle was built. Their label became more than just a brand; it became a reflection of their shared values and aspirations. Inspired by India's rich cultural tapestry, they sought to weave tradition and innovation together, creating pieces that celebrated diversity and inclusivity.

Navigating the intricate world of fashion, they were driven by a deep sense of purpose. Their label, comprising scarves, dupattas, and fashion jewelry, became a platform for amplifying marginalized voices and challenging stereotypes. Through initiatives like their Fashion for a Cause events, they endeavored to create spaces where everyone felt seen and heard, regardless of their background or identity.

One of their proudest moments came in 2019 when they showcased the LGBTQIA+ community in India through their fashion show. By featuring LGBTQIA+ models in their collections, they aimed to not only celebrate their beauty and talent but also to advocate for greater visibility and representation in the fashion industry.

The onset of the 2020 pandemic brought unprecedented challenges, but it also presented them with an opportunity to reaffirm their commitment to social activism. Through H1927, they launched initiatives to raise awareness and funds for critical causes, demonstrating the transformative power of fashion as a force for good and meaningful change.

Reflecting on the events leading up to that unforgettable evening at Beaux in San Francisco, where David Perry—the creator, host, and producer of *10 Percent*, the longest-running LGBT TV show in Northern California history—interviewed Prince Manvendra and Duke DeAndre for a charity event benefiting LGBTQIA+ causes in India, memories flood their minds, each carrying its own weight of significance and emotion.

Growing up in India, navigating his identity as a member of the LGBTQIA+ community was a daunting task for Prince Manvendra. The weight of societal expectations bore down on him, and the journey to self-acceptance was filled with obstacles. However, amidst those struggles, fate intervened, and he crossed paths with Duke DeAndre, forever altering the course of their lives. Their meeting was serendipitous, their connection immediate and profound. What drew Prince Manvendra to the duke was not just his magnetic personality, but the way he saw him for who he truly was, without judgment or reservation. In DeAndre's presence, Prince Manvendra found solace and acceptance, a sanctuary in a world fraught with uncertainty.

Their love story unfolded against the backdrop of their shared commitment to LGBTQIA+ rights and activism. Together, they embarked on a journey fueled by their passion for social change, each step deepening their bond and solidifying their partnership.

As they look back on that evening at Beaux, memories of the people they met flood back. It was there that Matthew Devlen, a pivotal figure in their journey, introduced them to two representatives of Amaranter, a fraternal order of Swedish knights founded in 1653 by Queen Christina of Sweden, at Epiphany. Asad Shah and Diane Weissmuller, sent by Matthew, made their debut at the fundraiser, marking the first of many encounters with Amaranter in the year to come, bringing a unique energy to the event and infusing it with enthusiasm and connection.

Surrounded by friends and supporters, Prince Manvendra and Duke DeAndre felt an overwhelming sense of gratitude for the opportunity to share their story and raise awareness for causes dear to their hearts. David Perry's insightful interview delved into the depths of their experiences and beliefs, serving as a powerful reminder of the importance of using their platform to effect positive change.

Looking ahead to their upcoming interview on *10 Percent*, they were filled with anticipation and excitement. It presented another chance to amplify their voices and shed light on the challenges facing the LGBTQIA+ community in India. Through open and honest dialogue, they hope to inspire others to join them in their fight for equality and justice.

Mingling with members of the MAX community, a social community for gay men and their friends, they were struck by the warmth and hospitality that surrounded them. The atmosphere was vibrant with laughter and conversation, creating an ideal setting for meaningful connections to flourish. It was heartening to see the spirit of inclusivity and acceptance that permeated the event. Whether sharing stories over cocktails or engaging in lively discussions about shared interests, each interaction felt genuine and uplifting. Throughout the evening, they were reminded of the importance of community and the power of connection. In a world where LGBTQIA+ individuals often face discrimination and marginalization, spaces like MAX provide a sanctuary where they can be themselves without fear or judgment.

Reflecting on their time with the MAX community, they were delighted to present the fabulous trunk show of H1927 scarves, with proceeds benefiting the LGBTQIA+ community campus ashram Rajpipla (QueerBagh) guesthouse. It was heartwarming to see the MAX community come together to support such an important cause, further reinforcing the power of unity and solidarity within their community. They are filled with gratitude for the opportunity to be a part of such a vibrant and supportive network. It is events like these that remind them of the strength and resilience of the LGBTQIA+ community and inspire them to continue their work towards a more inclusive and equitable world.

As Duke DeAndre and Prince Manvendra continue their journey together, they are grateful for every moment, every challenge, and every triumph they share. Their love is a testament to the resilience of the human spirit, a beacon of hope in a world often fraught with uncertainty. And as they navigate life's highs and lows, they do so with the wisdom of love guiding their path, illuminating the way forward with its gentle embrace.

Prince Manvendra and Duke DeAndre vividly recall their experience in Mauritius, an island nation in the Indian Ocean, renowned for its stunning beaches, lagoons, and reefs. Amidst its mountainous interior lies the Black River Gorges National Park, teeming with rainforests, waterfalls, and diverse wildlife like the flying fox. The capital, Port Louis, boasts attractions such as the Champs de Mars horse track, Eureka plantation house, and the eighteenth-century Sir Seewoosagur Ramgoolam Botanic Garden.

Upon arrival, stringent security measures were evident at the airport, with police and security personnel ensuring a fortified defense. Throughout their stay, Prince Manvendra and Duke DeAndre were accompanied by a dedicated team of security personnel, providing them with a sense of safety amidst uncertainty.

In 2017, Mauritius made history by organizing its first-ever Gay Pride event, spread over two consecutive days in the capital, Port Louis. Despite the presence of anti-LGBTQIA+ groups, Gay Pride was a resounding success. The LGBTQIA+ community in Mauritius is represented by two organizations: the Rainbow Collective (Collectif Arc-en-Ciel) and PILS (Prévention Information Lutte contre le SIDA, which translates to Prevention Information Fight against AIDS).

The Rainbow Collective, founded in 2005, advocates against homophobia and discrimination based on sexual orientation. PILS, established in 1996, serves as a vital center in Port Louis, focusing on educating and treating individuals with HIV/AIDS. Despite strides in LGBTQIA+ rights, concerns about safety persist, with reports of kidnappings, especially at night.

During their visit, Prince Manvendra and Duke DeAndre were guests of the Rainbow Collective, invited to attend the Pride events. Despite the security concerns, Duke DeAndre found solace in the picturesque beaches, enjoying morning walks along the shore near their beachfront hotel.

The hospitality they received was exceptional, and they were thrilled to be among talented individuals from the LGBTQIA+ community. However, their experience was not without its challenges. The looming threat from a radical Islamic group heightened their awareness of security protocols.

Despite meticulous planning, an incident occurred during the Pride parade when protesters breached barriers, prompting a swift response from local authorities. The experience underscored the importance of security and safety in navigating potential threats, reaffirming their commitment to fostering a world where safety, security, and inclusivity prevail.

In reflecting on the unforgettable experience of appearing on the Kardashians' show, vivid memories flood back for Prince Manvendra and Duke DeAndre, each painting a picture of fascinating events. Prince Manvendra received an invitation to Kim's Beverly Hills home, where he met Kim's children and filmed a lunch scene with the sisters Kendall, Kourtney, Kim, and Khloé. Meanwhile, Duke DeAndre found himself chased by paparazzi from Kim's house to the Hotel Bel-Air, eventually joining the family to conclude the filming at Kris's Calabasas home. During the gathering, Duke DeAndre had the privilege of tying an H1927 scarf gifted to Kris from them in a turban style and applying a red mark on her forehead, symbolizing honor, love, and prosperity in Hinduism. The mirrored floor in the living room captured their attention, leading to delightful moments of jumping up and down on it, sharing smiles and laughter.

Despite Duke DeAndre's active involvement, none of the footage featuring him made it into the episode of *Keeping Up with the Kardashians*. Prince Manvendra's filming made it into Season 13,

Episode 13 of *Keeping Up with the Kardashians*. Prince Manvendra and Duke DeAndre cherish the kindness and authenticity displayed by the Kardashian family. Kris also generously gifted them her cookbook *In the Kitchen with Kris* and Chrissy Teigen's cookbook *Cravings*, further enhancing the warmth of their encounter.

This encounter with the Kardashians exemplifies the wisdom of love, transcending boundaries of fame and culture to foster understanding, compassion, and acceptance. Through genuine connections and shared experiences, they pave the way for a more inclusive and empathetic world. Let us continue to champion love and acceptance in all its forms, recognizing that kindness and compassion know no bounds.

Meeting Belinda Carlisle and her son, James Duke Mason, was a delightful experience that intertwined their shared passions for activism and advocacy. Belinda, known for her impactful work in India, exuded warmth and genuine kindness as Prince Manvendra and Duke DeAndre gathered for lunch in Hollywood. Her unwavering support for LGBTQIA+ rights, particularly after James Duke Mason bravely came out at age fourteen, resonated deeply with Prince Manvendra. It was a testament to her compassion and commitment to creating a more inclusive world.

In 2014, Belinda co-founded Animal People Alliance, a non-profit organization based in Calcutta, India, dedicated to raising funds and empowering impoverished women to care for street animals. Her dedication to both animal welfare and social justice showcased her multifaceted approach to activism. As they engaged in conversation, Prince Manvendra was struck by her passion and drive to make a difference, not only in the lives of animals but also in the broader community.

Prince Manvendra had been working for animal rights since childhood, which brought him in touch with Belinda Carlisle, who used to visit India to spread awareness about violence against farm animals. Belinda had conducted one such campaign on donkeys who were being ill-treated and made to carry heavy loads of material. Prince Manvendra put Belinda in touch with other animal rights activists in India to strengthen her campaign. After marriage,

Prince Manvendra introduced Duke DeAndre to Belinda when they met for dinner in Mumbai.

James Duke Mason, with his vibrant energy and creative spirit, added another layer of depth to their encounter. As an actor and producer, he brought a unique perspective to their discussion, infusing it with insights from his experiences in the entertainment industry. Despite his busy schedule, James Duke Mason remained grounded and genuine, embodying the values of empathy and authenticity that are central to their shared mission of advocacy.

Their lunch with Belinda and James Duke Mason was more than just a casual meeting; it was an opportunity to forge meaningful connections and exchange ideas about how they could collectively drive positive change in the world. There were moments of laughter and camaraderie as Belinda shared stories and discussed how she traveled across India in an auto-rickshaw, also known to some as a "tuk-tuk," to raise awareness about the exploitation of donkeys. It was a reminder of the power of community and collaboration in advancing social causes.

As they parted ways, Prince Manvendra and Duke DeAndre couldn't help but feel inspired by Belinda and James Duke Mason's unwavering dedication to making a difference. Their courage to stand up for what they believe in, whether advocating for LGBTQIA+ rights or championing animal welfare, left a lasting impression on them. In their actions, the couple saw echoes of the wisdom of love—the belief that through empathy, compassion, and action, they can create a world that is more just, inclusive, and compassionate for all.

In August 2017, Prince Manvendra and Duke DeAndre embarked on a transformative journey to Las Vegas, Nevada, attending the National Gay and Lesbian Chamber of Commerce (NGLCC) Business and Leadership Conference. This significant event brought together LGBTQIA+ community members and global business leaders, marking a step forward for inclusivity and acceptance.

Among the distinguished keynote speakers whom Prince Manvendra and Duke DeAndre met were fashion icon and best-selling author Tim Gunn, entrepreneur and LGBTQIA+ advocate Lisa Vanderpump, CEO and author of *Predictable Success* Les McKeown, and investment experts Heidi Lehmann and David Beatty. Additionally, they met out CEO and philanthropist Mitchell Gold who graced the event with his presence, emphasizing the importance of unity and advocacy in advancing LGBTQIA+ rights on a global scale.

During the conference, Prince Manvendra shared his personal journey and advocacy work in India, stressing the need to raise awareness about LGBTQIA+ issues. Meanwhile, Duke DeAndre showcased the progress made in the United States regarding LGBTQ+ rights while acknowledging the ongoing work needed in this field.

The conference provided a platform for them to showcase their scarf collection from their private label, H1927 (Fashion for a Cause). The proceeds from this collection benefited the Lakshya Trust and the LGBTQIA+ community campus ashram (QueerBagh) in Gujarat, India, empowering the LGBTQIA+ community.

Their participation symbolized a pivotal moment in the global LGBTQIA+ movement, demonstrating unity and optimism as they advocated for LGBTQIA+ rights in both India and the United States. Amidst the conference buzz, Prince Manvendra and Duke DeAndre had the honor of meeting Dennis Shepard, father of Matthew Shepard, a young student whose tragic murder in 1998 became a symbol of hate crimes against the LGBTQIA+ community. The encounter with Dennis Shepard further reinforced their commitment to their advocacy efforts, reminding them of the importance of fighting for equality and acceptance for all.

This experience underscored the wisdom of love, showing that through unity, empathy, and advocacy, positive change can be achieved and barriers broken down. It reaffirmed their belief that by standing together and amplifying their voices, they could create a more inclusive and compassionate world for everyone, regardless of sexual orientation or gender identity.

In the heart of Hollywood, California, Prince Manvendra interrupted their conversation, excitement gleaming in his eyes as he showed Duke DeAndre a photo of three adorable kittens. His words were filled with warmth and compassion as he shared how these little furballs were in need of a loving home. Instantly drawn to the charm of one of the orange kittens, Duke DeAndre couldn't help but agree that they should bring one back with them to Mumbai when they returned.

Learning of the kittens' past, where two of their litter had tragically disappeared into a car engine compartment, Prince Manvendra couldn't bear to separate the remaining trio. To Duke DeAndre's surprise, he returned home with all three kittens in tow.

As they entered their lives, these furry bundles of joy quickly became known as "the brats." Tony, with his gentle demeanor and soft meow, became Prince Manvendra's steadfast companion, often found curled up on his stomach. Hercules, larger than his siblings and sporting a grouchy attitude, found solace in perching atop the wooden cupboards, observing the world with a watchful eye. And then there was Hissy, aptly named for her penchant for hissing at just about everything.

Their home was filled with laughter and mischief as their fur babies brought joy into every corner of their lives. Tony passed away during the pandemic, and Hercules tragically perished in a flash flood in 2023, which devastated the natural animal population around the Royal Establishment Hanumanteshwar, where they had moved in 2017. Despite the loss of her brothers, Hissy remains by their side, her playful antics and demanding meows a constant reminder of the love and happiness their furry companions have brought into their lives.

Through the highs and lows, their bond with their fur babies has taught them the wisdom of love. Their unconditional affection and unwavering presence serve as a constant reminder of the joy that comes from opening their hearts to others, furry or otherwise. In their company, they find solace, laughter, and the enduring beauty of a love that knows no bounds.

6

Breaking Barriers

In January 2018, Prince Manvendra and Duke DeAndre found themselves immersed in the rich tapestry of history that binds the royal families of Rajpipla and Balasinor. Spanning over two centuries, their families' connection lies deep within the heart of the Rewa Kantha political agency, where their legacies intertwine.

The Balasinor royal lineage, tracing its roots to the esteemed Muslim Babi dynasty, shares a profound friendship with them, anchored by their mutual dedication to LGBTQIA+ rights. Prince Manvendra's role in introducing Princess Aaliya to the television world through the BBC show *Undercover Princesses* marked a significant moment, fostering cultural preservation and advocacy endeavors.

Tragically, the passing of Nawab Muhammed Salabatkhan II in January 2018 cast a somber shadow over the Balasinor royal family. Yet, amidst mourning, the coronation of his son as the tenth generation of Balasinor Nawabs at the Garden Palace stood as a testament to their enduring legacy. Their presence at the coronation, among many other royal families, marked Duke DeAndre's inaugural attendance at such an event, where they were accorded the status of a royal couple, participating in all the ceremonial rituals.

The coronation, blending Rajput and Islamic traditions, echoed the diverse cultural heritage of the region. Their bond with the

Balasinor royal family, as well as their friendship with the Sachin royal family, underscores the unifying force of shared values despite disparate backgrounds.

Despite historical disparities, the Rajpipla and Balasinor royal families have forged a close-knit relationship over time, united by a common language, culture, and history. This bond, further solidified by personal friendships, serves as a beacon of hope in a world too often divided by intolerance.

Their role as royals extends beyond mere friendship, as they leverage their platform to champion LGBTQIA+ rights globally. Through initiatives promoting cultural exchange and awareness, they strive to create a more inclusive society, guided by the wisdom of love and acceptance.

The enduring relationship between the Rajpipla and Balasinor royal families exemplifies the power of friendship and shared values. Their commitment to equality and justice, coupled with advocacy for LGBTQIA+ rights, serves as a ray of hope, transcending boundaries and fostering unity in a world marred by division.

Prince Manvendra and Duke DeAndre were honored to receive an invitation from the government of India to join Prince Manvendra's parents, the King and Queen of Rajpipla, and various government officials on the stage for the 2018 Republic Day parade and celebration. This momentous occasion left an indelible mark on their hearts as they sat amidst dignitaries and officials, filled with a profound sense of pride and achievement.

Republic Day, celebrated on January 26th every year to commemorate the adoption of the Indian constitution in 1950, is organized with processions on parade grounds in Rajpipla and other cities, except New Delhi where the parade occurs on the public road. The event begins with the district collector or magistrate, accompanied by the superintendent of police, hoisting the national flag while the national anthem plays. Following this, the collector and the police superintendent form the guard of honor in an open Jeep. Subsequently, the march-past consists of police, Home Guard, and forest rangers parading around the ground. The collector then delivers a speech from the podium before returning to sit in the audience. Following this, different floats representing departments such as the medical team, forest department, and agricultural department are paraded. Cultural activities organized by various schools follow, featuring patriotic songs, dances, and plays. Awards and honors are presented to various government departments and police officers, with schools also giving prizes for the best performances in cultural activities. The event concludes with the singing of the national anthem and a tree plantation drive by the dignitaries present.

Despite the absence of legal recognition for same-sex marriage in India, Prince Manvendra and Duke DeAndre's inclusion in such a significant event spoke volumes about the strides made in terms of LGBTQIA+ rights and societal acceptance. They were deeply impressed by the royal family and establishment's innovative approach to embracing Duke DeAndre's presence, reflecting their commitment to inclusivity and diversity.

Witnessing the grandeur of the parade and celebration unfold before them, they were captivated by the rich tapestry of cultures, languages, and traditions that define India. It served as a poignant reminder of the beauty inherent in the country's diversity and the unity that emerges when people from all walks of life come together to celebrate shared heritage and values.

Leaving the event, they were filled with a profound sense of inspiration and optimism for the future. While acknowledging the ongoing challenges faced by the LGBTQIA+ community in terms of rights and acceptance, events like these serve as beacons of hope, demonstrating that progress is indeed within reach. They are immensely grateful for the opportunity to have participated in such a significant occasion and remain steadfast in their commitment to fostering a more inclusive and accepting society, guided by the enduring wisdom of love.

In February 2018, Duke DeAndre and Prince Manvendra found themselves immersed in the esteemed ambiance of the India Business Group (IBG), where they stood as honored members among a vibrant community of like-minded individuals. Being part of IBG, within the modern Chamber of Commerce, was more than just a membership—it was an affirmation of their commitment to progress and prosperity, guided by the wisdom of love.

The transformative journey of IBG was steered by a diverse board of committee members, each representing a spectrum of business expertise and individual perspectives. This diversity ensured a comprehensive and inclusive approach, guiding the chamber towards continual progress and excellence, all under the guiding light of love.

In a moment brimming with significance, Mr. Vikash Mittersain, the esteemed president of IBG, honored Duke DeAndre and Prince Manvendra with the prestigious NGO/Public Service award at the inaugural IBG Awards of Excellence in February 2018. This accolade stood as a testament to their noteworthy contributions to public service and their steadfast dedication to making a positive impact within the community.

Feeling immensely proud, the duo realized that this was the first time they, as a gay couple, had received acknowledgement from a business group that was not solely focused on LGBTQIA+ issues. To be celebrated at this level in the business world in India was an achievement in itself, highlighting the progress towards inclusivity and acceptance.

Receiving the award as a couple was a deeply meaningful experience, as it allowed them to be visible members of the business community while honoring their authentic selves. Through their involvement with IBG, their journey became intertwined with a commitment to excellence, service, and a shared vision for a thriving future, all guided by the wisdom of love.

In their shared journey, Prince Manvendra and Duke DeAndre have encountered myriad challenges and moments of profound joy that have left an indelible mark on their lives. One such pivotal decision they faced revolved around the vehicle fleet at the Royal Establishment of Hanumanteshwar. As their vehicles aged and safety concerns emerged, they embarked on a journey of deliberation and reflection.

Turning to meditation, a practice they often engage in to seek clarity and guidance, Duke DeAndre and Prince Manvendra delved deep into their hearts and minds. Through this introspective process, they arrived at the decision to sell the fleet and channel the funds towards the development of the LGBTQIA+ community campus ashram in Rajpipla.

As they downsized the fleet, their focus shifted towards finding a new vehicle that aligned with their needs and values. Initially considering an SUV, a serendipitous encounter during a visit to the temple unveiled a seven-seater Datsun that seemed tailor-made for their requirements. Guided by the divine presence of Harsiddhi Mataji, the goddess of the royal family of Rajpipla, they felt a profound sense of reassurance in their decision-making process.

Their relationship with the goddess holds deep significance in their lives, offering them solace and direction in times of uncertainty. Despite the trials they've faced as partners, their bond has remained unshakeable, rooted in mutual respect, understanding, and love. Prince Manvendra's tireless advocacy for LGBTQIA+ rights, despite personal challenges, and Duke DeAndre's unwavering support are testaments to their commitment to their community's well-being.

The decision to invest in the LGBTQIA+ community campus is emblematic of their dedication to creating safe havens and nurturing inclusivity. The acquisition of the Datsun not only serves as a practical mode of transportation but also symbolizes their unwavering commitment to serving the community.

As Prince Manvendra set foot on the bustling streets of Amsterdam, excitement and anticipation surged within him. Representing the AIDS Healthcare Foundation as its Brand Ambassador, he embarked on a journey to participate in the international conference on HIV/AIDS in July 2018. It was a profound honor for him to represent not only the organization but also his country, Gujarat State, and he was eager to both share his experiences and learn from others.

Accompanied by the India team, he navigated the conference venue, feeling the weight of responsibility as the sole representative from their organization focused on HIV/AIDS issues in Gujarat. Surrounded by delegates from diverse backgrounds, including government officials and political representatives, he found comfort in the familiar faces among them, fostering a sense of camaraderie. During the conference, he had the privilege of delivering a presentation on the LGBTQIA+ community campus ashram under development at the Royal Establishment of Hanumanteshwar. It was a moment to showcase their progress and articulate their vision for the future before a diverse and influential audience.

But his time in Amsterdam wasn't confined to professional engagements alone. He also took part in a march protesting against the pharmaceutical companies' practices of raising drug prices, boldly amplifying their message with the slogan "Pharma Greed Kills." Furthermore, he immersed himself in the local community's work by volunteering in AHF Amsterdam's clinic, mobile testing van, and office, contributing meaningfully to their efforts.

Amidst these activities, Prince Manvendra received a gracious invitation from Mayor Femke Halsema to a dinner party at her residence, where he engaged in enlightening conversations with fellow LGBTQIA+ activists from around the world. It was humbling for him to exchange experiences and ideas with such inspiring individuals, reaffirming the interconnectedness of their global community and the wisdom of love that unites them.

During the Pride celebrations, he stood before a large audience, delivering a public speech that was accentuated by the surreal setting of a chariot ride, adorned in regal attire. The overwhelming outpouring of love and support enveloped him as he navigated the festivities, surrounded by drag queens and AHF's float on the canal.

Throughout Pride, Prince Manvendra maintained the traditional Indian "Namaste" gesture, receiving cheers and respect from the audience—a poignant reminder of the power of cultural exchange and the enduring wisdom of love. Additionally, he had the pleasure of reconnecting with HH Prince Remigius of Jaffna, Sri Lanka, with whom he had shared the experience of participating in the BBC reality show *Undercover Princes* in 2008, highlighting the interconnectedness of their journeys.

One pivotal moment in their journey unfolded in 2018 as they embarked on a transformative voyage to Hong Kong for the

Human Dignity Festival, queering the seventieth anniversary of the Universal Declaration of Human Rights with its second annual human rights conference. Held in collaboration with NGO Planet Ally, the festival featured seven international speakers and seventy NGOs to speak on LGBTQIA+ issues and human rights.

"Human dignity is the right to live one's truth and have the freedom to be who you are," said Prince Manvendra, one of the Human Dignity Festival's speakers.

At the festival, they were invited to speak, allowing them to weave their narratives as LGBTQIA+ individuals and advocates for change. They emphasized the profound impact of love and acceptance in shaping a more equitable society, rallying others to join them in their quest for equality.

Beyond the festival, they attended a fashion event organized by H1927, where Duke DeAndre served as the creative director. This installment of the label's Fashion for a Cause series was particularly meaningful, as it aimed to raise awareness and funds for important social issues.

The runway showcased avant-garde designs inspired by Hong Kong's vibrant culture, each piece a testament to the label's commitment to pushing the boundaries of conventional fashion. Yet, what truly set this event apart was its unwavering focus on social causes—with proceeds directed towards local organizations championing LGBTQIA+ rights and fostering acceptance.

Participating in the event was an honor, allowing them to passionately advocate for the transformative power of fashion in driving social change. They urged attendees to embrace greater acceptance and understanding of LGBTQIA+ individuals, encouraging them to support organizations dedicated to equality and human rights.

Their time in Hong Kong etched itself as a poignant reminder of the importance of standing firm in their convictions. From marching in the Gay Pride Parade to vocally condemning banned books, they remained steadfast in their commitment to creating a more inclusive and accepting world.

In their journey as royals, Prince Manvendra and Duke DeAndre discovered the intricate dance of love, courage, and advocacy.

Through the highs and lows, they found strength within their bond and an unwavering commitment to champion acceptance and equality for all.

One sunny afternoon in December 2018, the warmth of Mumbai embraced Prince Manvendra and Duke DeAndre as they embarked on an unexpected adventure. It all began with a call from Viraj Singh, the talented cinematographer, and relative of Prince Manvendra. His invitation to meet Violet Chachki, a renowned figure in the LGBTQIA+ community, filled them with excitement and curiosity. Despite their initial unfamiliarity with Violet, a quick online search revealed her remarkable presence and influence.

Joined by Dr. Samarpan Maiti—Mr. Gay India, who happened to be in Mumbai at the time—they eagerly accepted the opportunity to meet Violet and take part in a filming session for the Violet documentary. As they made their way to the beach for the shoot, the buzz of anticipation filled the air. Violet's magnetic energy drew a crowd as they walked, her charisma lighting up their surroundings.

Throughout the day, amidst the hustle and bustle of filming, they found themselves immersed in the wisdom of love. It was a reminder of the interconnectedness of their LGBTQIA+ family on a global scale—a bond that transcends geographical boundaries and cultural differences. In Violet's presence, surrounded by like-minded individuals, they felt a sense of belonging and unity that filled their hearts with joy.

As the sun dipped below the horizon, casting a golden glow over the Mumbai skyline, they reflected on the significance of moments like these. They serve as reminders of the power of community, of coming together to celebrate their shared identities and experiences. In the warmth of Mumbai's embrace, they found not only camaraderie but also a deeper understanding of the transformative power of love.

As Prince Manvendra and Duke DeAndre reminisce about that unforgettable day, the vibrant spirit of San Francisco's streets still thrums with excitement in their hearts. Sponsored by Salesforce, their journey was filled with a week-long series of events, starting with an exclusive dinner with Salesforce leadership. Prince

Manvendra's keynote speech at the Salesforce Pride event held at their headquarters in San Francisco was a highlight, where they shared their experiences and insights on LGBTQIA+ rights.

Marching alongside the Salesforce team in the San Francisco Gay Pride Parade was an extraordinary experience. As they walked in front of the float adorned with drag performers, they felt a deep sense of pride and solidarity. Handing out stickers and gifts to the thousands of onlookers lining the streets added to the joy of the occasion, making it even more memorable.

For them, the parade meant much more than just revelry; it was a platform to amplify their voices for change. They relished the chance to connect with leaders from various LGBTQIA+ organizations, sharing their own stories of triumph over adversity and underscoring the timeless importance of acceptance and love.

Standing shoulder to shoulder with the LGBTQIA+ community of California and beyond, they felt an overwhelming sense of pride and solidarity. While acknowledging the road ahead, they embraced the hope kindled by such gatherings—hope for a world where equality reigns supreme.

Looking back on that cherished day, they're filled with gratitude for the privilege of being part of history in the making. It's a poignant reminder that no matter their backgrounds, each of them holds the power to make a difference, to champion equality, and to stand firm in their beliefs. As long as they continue to raise their voices for acceptance and love, they're lighting the path toward a future where everyone belongs.

"Left to Right: HH Prince DeAndre, Duke of Hanumanteshwar; HRH Crown Prince Manvendra Singh Gohil of Rajpipla; HRH Maharaja Raghubir Singh Gohil of Rajpipla, attending the wedding of Prince Shivendra Singh of Jaisalmer."

"Prince Manvendra and Duke DeAndre standing on a terrace at Mandir Palace, attending the wedding of Prince Shivendra Singh of Jaisalmer."

"Left to Right: Maharaja Raghubir Singh Gohil of Rajpipla, Duke DeAndre, Prince Manvendra Singh Gohil, Maharaja Aishwarya Pratap Singh Chauhan of Chota Udepur attending the wedding of Himmat Singh Jadeja's son in Vapi, Gujarat, India."

"Left to right: Duke DeAndre, Lisa Vanderpump, Prince Manvendra, William Kapfer at the NGLCC event, 15th annual NGLCC International Business and Leadership Conference at Caesars Palace, Las Vegas, Nevada."

"Award ceremony by the India Business Group where Prince Manvendra and Duke DeAndre accepted the award together as an openly gay couple."

"Prince Manvendra and Duke DeAndre attending a function hosted by Mimi and Shamee in Mumbai, India

"Prince Manvendra with a shaved head during the Mundan ceremony following the passing of Granny, a Hindu tradition where male family members shave their heads in mourning."

"Prince Manvendra and Duke DeAndre pose for a couples' photo with the Royal Photographer in Rajpipla, Gujarat."

"Prince Manvendra and Duke DeAndre heading to the World AIDS event hosted by AHF India Cares in Mumbai, India."

"Prince Manvendra and Duke DeAndre visiting Lakhtar Fort City and meeting HRH Thakur Balbhadra Singh, brother of Rani Jayendra Kumari of Rajpipla (Granny)."

"Prince Manvendra and Kris Jenner after Duke DeAndre gifted Kris a H1927 scarf, which he also used to tie a turban on her head and place a bindi on her forehead. Traditionally, the bindi is placed on the sixth chakra, ajna, symbolizing concealed wisdom and enhancing concentration, also representing the third eye."

"Left to Right: Duke DeAndre, David Harrison Levi, Prince Manvendra at the Richerette fashion show by Richie Rich at Beverly Hilton, Art Hearts Fashion LAFW, Beverly Hills, CA."

"Celebrating San Francisco Pride with Salesforce! From left to right: Tony Prophet (Chief Equality Officer, Salesforce), Anke Hebig Prophet (Board Member, Women's HIV Program SF Bay Area), front left Duke DeAndre, Parker Harris (Co-Founder, Salesforce & CTO, Slack), and Prince Manvendra."

"Prince Manvendra and Duke DeAndre at the LA Pride Parade, riding in a convertible Mustang."

"Broadway to Bombay event hosted by Prince Manvendra and Duke DeAndre at the King's Place in Rajpipla."

PART 3

EXPANDING HORIZONS (2019-2020)

7
Cultural Connections

As Duke DeAndre and Prince Manvendra found themselves barricaded in the tower of the Hanumanteshwar estate, fear gripped Duke DeAndre's heart like never before. Outside, the atmosphere was charged with tension as enraged villagers demanded control of acres of land for farming. Their voices grew louder, their demands more insistent, and the couple knew they were facing a volatile situation. Surrounded by the protective walls of the estate, they braced themselves for what could unfold next.

The estate's management shared their concern, recognizing the potential for violence in the villagers' agitation. Locked in the tower, they felt a mixture of anxiety and determination to ensure their own safety and that of those around them.

In a moment of urgency, they turned to social media, hoping to attract the attention of the authorities. Their hearts sank as their initial calls for help were redirected, the police preoccupied with preparations for the prime minister's visit. But undeterred, they persisted, making call after call until they finally reached the ears of those who could help.

When the police finally arrived, their presence diffused the tension, and the villagers dispersed without further incident. However, the police informed the villagers that this was a matter for the courts, and they would need to file a complaint against the establishment. They were also told not to come back to the estate, as it was a civil matter.

Yet, the episode left a lasting impression, highlighting gaps in their security measures and the need for better communication channels during emergencies.

Throughout the ordeal, Duke DeAndre and Prince Manvendra remained resolute, ensuring not only their own safety but also that of the estate's staff. Their actions spoke volumes about the kind of leadership needed in moments of crisis—calm, decisive, and focused on protecting those in their care.

As they reflect on that harrowing experience, they are reminded of the importance of preparedness and swift action in the face of adversity. Their bond, fortified by love and trust, gave them the strength to navigate the storm together. And while the scars of that day may linger, they serve as a testament to their resilience and their unwavering commitment to each other's well-being.

In June 2019, amidst the bustling energy of New York City, Prince Manvendra and Duke DeAndre embarked on a transformative journey at the Human Rights Conference: World Pride 2019. From June 24th–25th, they immersed themselves in the human rights conference hosted by New York Law School (NYLS) in Tribeca, a pivotal gathering where advocates from around the world converged to address pressing issues facing the LGBTQIA+ community. The World Pride 2019 Human Rights Conference featured forty panels and over two hundred speakers, including esteemed NYLS faculty members.

During this event, Prince Manvendra and Duke DeAndre seized the opportunity to engage with a diverse array of voices and perspectives, contributing to the global dialogue on LGBTQIA+ rights. The conference served as a platform for activists, artists, policymakers, and educators to shine a light on the challenges facing the global LGBTQIA+ community.

Amidst the gathering of thought leaders and changemakers, Prince Manvendra and Duke DeAndre were inspired by the opportunity to exchange ideas and insights, seeing many familiar faces from the Human Dignity Festival and further solidifying their commitment to advocacy and activism. It was during this conference that they had the privilege of meeting media consultant Cathy Renna, an influential figure in LGBTQIA+ PR and communications.

As advocates from around the world gathered to champion equality for all families, the atmosphere crackled with unity and purpose. Prince Manvendra and Duke DeAndre stood alongside fellow defenders of human rights, feeling a surge of optimism knowing that their collective voices had the power to effect change. Amidst moments of camaraderie and solidarity, they were reminded that in the fight for equality, they were stronger together, drawing strength from their shared purpose and passion.

Prince Manvendra's relationship with Jessica Stern dates back to 2016 when he was invited to speak at OutRight International in New York. Both Prince Manvendra and Jessica have been actively involved in working on human rights issues in the LGBTQIA+ community. They were both part of a panel discussion for the Human Rights Conference in New York. But before they entered the auditorium to address the audience, they had a private talk about the developments in India since they met in 2016. Prince Manvendra informed Jessica of the major milestone that happened in 2018, with the Supreme Court decriminalizing homosexuality in India. He informed Jessica that the implementation of this legal change had been very slow and that he had increased his advocacy, especially in educational institutions creating awareness amongst students. Jessica assured Prince Manvendra of any help he needed on an international platform.

Stepping onto the stage at the World Pride event in New York City in 2019, Duke DeAndre felt a swell of emotions flood his heart. Alongside him stood his husband, Prince Manvendra, and together, they embodied not only the representation of the LGBTQIA+ community but also a shared dedication to advocacy and activism. Their journey to World Pride was a testament to their commitment to the cause.

Their experiences during World Pride were truly extraordinary and left an indelible mark on their souls. Among the most profound moments was the culmination of the filming of *Pieces of Us*, where all the subjects of the film united to march in the World Pride parade. Standing shoulder to shoulder with others, their hearts beat as one in their collective fight for equality and acceptance. Riding on the float with Swish Ally Fund during the NYC Pride March was an unforgettable highlight, enveloped in the electrifying energy of the crowd and the pulsating rhythm of the music.

During their time in New York City, they were thrilled to participate in a fundraiser hosted by Rodrigo Salem and Carla Fine in Chelsea, Manhattan. Under the emcee Joshua Patel's guidance, the event aimed to support both the Lakshya Trust and the LGBTQIA+ community campus ashram Rajpipla (QueerBagh). Witnessing the generosity of the attendees as they united to raise funds for causes close to their hearts was profoundly touching.

The sheer scale of World Pride NYC was staggering, with an estimated five million people attending events in Manhattan during the final weekend alone, making it the largest LGBTQIA+ Pride event ever held. Surrounded by a vibrant and diverse community, all exuding love and acceptance, they were enveloped in an overwhelming sense of unity and solidarity.

Each moment they shared during the event served as a powerful testament to the resilience, acceptance, and love that defines the LGBTQIA+ community, transcending geographical boundaries and cultural differences. In every interaction and at every event, they were reminded of the transformative power of love, guiding them through their journey with unwavering strength and compassion.

Riding the float was an emotional experience, heightened by the presence of other participants in the documentary *Pieces of Us*. As the film crew captured their moments of joy, wonder, excitement, and grief, they felt a deep sense of connection with each other and with the broader LGBTQIA+ community. Together, they experienced a range of emotions, from jubilation to introspection, as they celebrated their identities and shared their stories.

Participating in the festivities alongside Matthew Devlen and the invitation to the Amaranter Ball in Sweden were highlights that added layers of depth to their experiences, reinforcing the interconnectedness of their global community and reaffirming the wisdom of love that binds them all together.

The event itself was a celebration of diversity, acceptance, and solidarity, bringing together individuals from all walks of life to embrace and champion LGBTQIA+ rights. It was a moment of profound connection and solidarity, marking a meaningful milestone in their ongoing journey as advocates for equality and inclusion.

In August 2019, as Prince Manvendra and Duke DeAndre embarked on their journey to the Global Vipassana Pagoda, Duke DeAndre couldn't contain his excitement. The tales he'd heard about this magnificent structure filled him with anticipation, eager to immerse himself in the promised tranquility. While only Duke DeAndre attended the ten-day Vipassana Meditation course that August, he couldn't wait to share every detail of his experience with Prince Manvendra.

Entering the pagoda, Duke DeAndre was awestruck by its sheer size and magnificence. The grand structure housed bone relics of Gautama Buddha, making it the world's largest hollow stone masonry structure containing Buddha relics. Multiple domes, including the grand central dome, stood atop the first dome, creating a breathtaking sight. Inside, the vast meditation hall spanned over 6000 square meters, accommodating more than eight thousand practitioners, all seeking the transformative power of Vipassana meditation as taught by Mr. S. N. Goenka.

As Duke DeAndre settled in for meditation, a profound sense of calm enveloped him, guided by the wisdom of love. The technique, taught during the ten-day residential courses, offered a path to inner peace and self-discovery. The absence of fees for these courses, funded entirely by donations from those who had benefited, underscored the altruistic spirit of Vipassana's teachings. The pagoda complex itself stood as a testament to gratitude for Buddha's teachings, providing a sanctuary for practitioners seeking solace and insight.

In the silence of meditation, Duke DeAndre felt a deep connection to something beyond himself, guided by the wisdom of love. The experience was profound, leaving an indelible mark on his soul. As he departed the Global Vipassana Pagoda, a newfound sense of peace and clarity accompanied him, illuminated by the wisdom of love. Duke DeAndre knew then that his journey with Vipassana would continue, enriched by sharing his experience with Prince Manvendra. With renewed purpose and gratitude for the transformative power of meditation, they ventured forth, guided by the boundless wisdom of love.

In August 2019, Prince Manvendra and Duke DeAndre received a significant invitation that would shape their journey. KPMG International Ltd., one of the Big Four accounting organizations, invited them to speak at their Mumbai office on the topic "LGBTQ in India—The Changing Landscape." Together, they eagerly prepared for the event, feeling a mix of excitement and determination in the air.

The theme of the engagement resonated deeply with them. It was about creating positive change, not just within workplaces but in communities and society at large. They understood that such change often requires a bold approach—challenging assumptions, speaking up for what's right, and taking decisive actions to foster inclusion. This wasn't just about delivering a speech; it was about advocating for a cause close to their hearts.

As they arrived at the KPMG office, a sense of anticipation enveloped them. The setting was professional yet welcoming, with attendees ranging from KPMG Global Services Leadership Group members to directors and above. The room buzzed with energy, and they knew they had an opportunity to make a meaningful impact.

Their engagement aimed to build connections with Community Business, an organization recognized for its commitment to advancing responsible and inclusive business practices in Asia. Additionally, it offered a platform to position themselves as thought leaders in front of a targeted audience of senior leadership at KPMG.

Behind the scenes, there were moments of reflection and preparation. They discussed their approach, ensuring that their message would resonate authentically with the audience. Each word they chose carried the weight of their shared experiences, their struggles, and their triumphs.

Standing before the participants, they felt a sense of purpose. They spoke from the heart, sharing their personal journeys, the challenges they faced, and the progress they've witnessed. It wasn't just about statistics or theories; it was about humanizing the LGBTQIA+ experience, making it relatable and tangible.

Throughout the engagement, there were nods of understanding, moments of empathy, and even a few tears. They knew they were reaching people, touching hearts, and perhaps sparking a newfound sense of awareness and compassion.

After the event, as they reflected on the experience, a profound sense of fulfillment washed over them. They had seized the opportunity to advocate for change, to challenge perceptions, and to inspire action. It was a reminder that even in the corporate world, there is space for empathy, understanding, and progress.

Looking back, that day at KPMG wasn't just about delivering a speech; it was about embodying the values of courage, resilience, and love. It was about standing tall and speaking their truth, knowing that every word had the power to make a difference in someone's life. And in that moment, they realized the true wisdom of love—the transformative power it holds to create a more inclusive and compassionate world.

8
Love Knows No Borders

In the captivating tapestry of their lives, Prince Manvendra and Duke DeAndre found themselves immersed in the remarkable presence of Brian Rusch. Their hearts brimmed with gratitude for the cherished moments spent with this extraordinary soul.

Prince Manvendra connected with Brian for the first time in 2018 through Facebook, where he saw Prince Manvendra on the page called "Queers of Note." During their conversation on Facebook, Brian expressed appreciation for Prince Manvendra's development of a module for a university in Gujarat State, to teach students about the issues of the LGBTQIA+ community. Prince Manvendra also shared with Brian his involvement as an AIDS Healthcare Foundation Brand Ambassador and his marriage to Duke DeAndre. Brian mentioned to Prince Manvendra that he is mostly based in San Francisco and that his husband works as a scientist at Gilead Sciences. At the beginning of 2020, Brian expressed his desire to visit Mumbai for the first time in his life and set up a plan to meet Prince Manvendra and Duke DeAndre.

As Brian's story unfolded before them, they were spellbound, not only by the layers of his identity but also by the kindness, gentleness, and generosity that emanated from him. From being the founder and Chief Executive Officer at Out for Equality to serving as Vice Chair of Diversity, Equity, and Inclusion on the Joint Advisory Council at Rotary International, and a Strategic Consultant at Kailash Satyarthi Children's Foundation—US, Brian's resume spoke volumes about his commitment to making the world a better place. Yet, beyond his impressive titles and accomplishments, it was his compassionate spirit and unwavering dedication to advocating for LGBTQIA+ rights that truly touched their hearts.

Seated in the rich fabric of their shared conversations, they delved into the intricate tapestry of Brian's tireless advocacy for LGBTQIA+ rights in India and worldwide. His gentle demeanor and genuine empathy created a space where they felt not only heard but also deeply understood. Together, they bore witness to the transformative impact of collaboration and activism, their voices resonating in harmony for a world that embraces diversity and inclusivity. In Brian, they found not just an ally, but also a friend whose kindness and wisdom of love left an indelible mark on their souls.

Their hearts swelled with pride as they reflected on the ripple effects of their collective efforts, reaching across borders to touch the lives of LGBTQIA+ individuals globally. In a moment of profound significance, Lakshya Trust and Out for Equality forged an official partnership in February 2023, cementing their joint commitment to advancing LGBTQIA+ rights and equality.

One particularly memorable day was when Duke DeAndre had the pleasure of showing Brian the wonders of Mumbai. They ventured to the Sanjay Gandhi National Park, an expansive 87 square kilometer (34 square mile) protected area adorned with the ancient Kanheri caves, sculpted by monks from rocky basaltic cliffs over 2400 years ago. This sanctuary, coupled with the iconic Global Vipassana Pagoda, holds both cultural and natural significance, drawing over two million visitors annually. Spending the day exploring Mumbai and sharing some of Duke DeAndre's favorite spots was an experience etched forever in their memories.

As they pen these words, their hearts overflow with gratitude for the unique connection they share with Brian. The promise of future reunions hangs in the air, beckoning a time when they can gather once more, continuing to script the narrative of love, acceptance, and the pursuit of equality, guided always by the enduring wisdom of love.

As Prince Manvendra and Duke DeAndre entered the familiar confines of the Royal Establishment of Hanumanteshwar in 2020, a palpable sense of unease settled upon them. Having recently returned from an international journey, they found themselves thrust into the midst of the unfolding crisis of the Covid-19 pandemic, a global calamity that had originated in China in December 2019 and rapidly spread worldwide.

Their return home was anything but ordinary. They were summoned back to attend a court proceeding regarding an ongoing legal dispute with villagers seeking access to the estate for farming. The tension surrounding the litigation compounded the already tumultuous atmosphere, exacerbated by the uncertainty and fear brought about by the pandemic.

The severity of the situation prompted the World Health Organization (WHO) to declare a Public Health Emergency of International Concern (PHEIC) on January 30th, 2020, eventually escalating to a pandemic declaration on March 11th, 2020. In response, the government dispatched a medical team to assess their health and implement quarantine measures as a precaution.

A quarantine sign at the front gate signaled their restricted status as they were confined within the estate's borders. The nationwide lockdown enforced strict isolation measures with their movements confined to the estate grounds and essential supplies meticulously provided, including food, water, and medical provisions.

During the prolonged lockdown, starting in March 2020, Prince Manvendra and Duke DeAndre found themselves under quarantine by government officials at the Royal Establishment of Hanumanteshwar. This confinement presented numerous challenges, lasting nearly five months due to the stringent regulations that restricted even essential movements such as food procurement.

As weeks turned into months, the isolation took its toll, compounded by the absence of loved ones. Yet, they recognized the imperative of collective safety in isolation, fully understanding the gravity of the global pandemic. Updates on the pandemic's progression served as sobering reminders of the shared struggle unfolding worldwide.

Amidst the trials, unexpected difficulties arose, such as the depletion of cat food for their beloved pets. With Amazon deliveries prohibited, they faced the prospect of their cats going hungry until a timely delivery of dog food from a member of the royal family included cat food as part of the essential items.

Another incident occurred during a trip to Rajpipla for essentials, during which they were unexpectedly questioned by government officers about their absence during an inspection visit to the establishment. Despite these challenges, their resolve to navigate the uncertainties of the pandemic together only grew stronger, underscored by their enduring bond.

In the face of adversity, their relationship flourished, strengthened by their unwavering love and commitment. As their isolation period drew to a close, they underwent Covid-19 testing, the negative results providing a welcome relief and a testament to the collective efforts that contained the virus's spread.

The pandemic prompted reflection and a newfound appreciation for life's simple joys. It imparted invaluable lessons on resilience and gratitude, reinforcing the fragility of human existence. Reunited with loved ones, they emerged from the ordeal with profound gratitude, cherishing each moment as a precious blessing.

Contemplating the tumultuous chapter etched in his family's history, Prince Manvendra finds solace in the profound wisdom of love that guided their journey. Amidst the trials, his thoughts invariably turn to the extraordinary fortitude exhibited by his lineage, particularly his revered father, HH Maharana Shri Raghubirsinhji Rajendrasinhji Sahib, the thirty-eighth direct descendant of the Gohil dynasty and the Maharaja of Rajpipla. Even as Covid-19 threatened his father's well-being and the looming specter of separation shadowed his cherished spouse, Duke DeAndre, Prince Manvendra found himself ensnared in the daunting web of adversity.

In such moments, familial bonds transcended personal strife. Despite any fissures with the establishment stemming from his advocacy for LGBTQIA+ rights, Prince Manvendra understood that love's wisdom dictated prioritizing familial duty over individual grievances. Thus, he resolved to stand resolute alongside the establishment and Duke DeAndre in their hour of need. Together, they embarked on an arduous quest to secure the finest medical care for Prince Manvendra's ailing father, securing his admission to the esteemed Bhailal Amin General Hospital in Vadodara, Gujarat.

Their journey was fraught with bureaucratic obstacles, particularly concerning Duke DeAndre's visa status. Yet, their unwavering commitment to familial unity propelled them forward, undeterred by the hurdles that threatened to derail their efforts. Theirs was a testament to the resilience of the human spirit, fueled by the transformative power of love that bound them together as a family.

Throughout the ordeal, love served as their guiding beacon, infusing their actions with compassion, empathy, and solidarity. It was a poignant lesson in transcending personal grievances for a higher purpose—the preservation of familial harmony and well-being. Anchored by their shared love and unwavering devotion, they weathered the tempest of uncertainty together, finding solace and strength amidst the chaos.

As Duke DeAndre faced pressure to depart from India and Prince Manvendra grappled with his father's health crisis, their bond remained unyielding. Despite the geographical distance separating them, Prince Manvendra remained vigilant in monitoring his father's health, overseeing his eventual recovery with Ayurveda and homeopathic treatments upon his return to the palace in Rajpipla.

In the end, victory emerged from the crucible of adversity. Prince Manvendra's father triumphed over illness, buoyed by the steadfast presence of Duke DeAndre by his side. Though their trials concluded, the echoes of their journey reverberated within their hearts, underscoring the enduring significance of resilience, determination, and the immutable force of love. Their story stands as a testament to the transformative power of familial love and solidarity, reminding us that even in the face of seemingly insurmountable challenges, love's wisdom prevails, illuminating the path forward with hope and resilience.

A Royal Commitment: Ten Years of Marriage and Activism

In 2020, Duke DeAndre and Prince Manvendra embarked on a journey rife with challenges, yet buoyed by the enduring strength of their love. Their bond, steeped in the wisdom of love, became a steadfast beacon, guiding them through life's twists and turns with unwavering resolve. Amidst their shared path's ebbs and flows, a serendipitous encounter with Adam Pasha—Bengaluru's celebrated stage dancer, and the city's first drag queen—added a captivating chapter to their narrative.

Prince Manvendra's introduction to Adam brought him into Duke DeAndre's orbit, as Adam sought their collaboration in envisioning an LGBTQIA+ community campus in Bengaluru. Eager to champion this cause, they extended their wholehearted support to Adam's vision, embracing the opportunity to contribute to a more inclusive future. Throughout the pandemic, Duke DeAndre and Adam cultivated a deep friendship, bridging the physical distance through heartfelt phone calls and animated video chats.

Adam's arrival in Rajpipla to celebrate Prince Manvendra's birthday in September 2020 infused their royal court with his infectious charm and vivacious energy. Despite the somber backdrop of the pandemic, Adam's presence brought a glimmer of joy to their lives, his vibrant spirit lifting their collective spirits. However, their happiness was tempered by the realities of their circumstances beginning to unfold.

Navigating the complexities of the Covid-19 pandemic, coupled with India's stringent visa regulations and the absence of legal recognition for same-sex marriages, presented Duke DeAndre with a formidable dilemma. As the government mandated his departure from the country, they grappled with the harsh reality of their union being unrecognized under Indian law. Yet, in the face of adversity, their bond only grew stronger, fortified by mutual support and unwavering devotion.

Their resilience faced another test when Adam found himself ensnared in a legal case, arrested under the stringent provisions of the Narcotic Drugs & Psychotropic Substances Act. The news sent shock waves through their hearts, leaving them reeling from the sudden upheaval. Despite the geographical distance separating them, Duke DeAndre and Prince Manvendra remained steadfast pillars of support for Adam, offering solace and assistance in whatever capacity they could.

Amidst the trials and tribulations, they found solace in the enduring embrace of friendship, recognizing its profound capacity to sustain them through life's darkest hours. As staunch advocates for LGBTQIA+ rights and creators of safe spaces, they drew strength from their shared identity, unwavering in their commitment to championing the community's cause.

Guided by the wisdom of love, their journey continues, a testament to the transformative power of authenticity and resilience. Through their story, they strive to inspire others to embrace their true selves unapologetically, fostering a world where love knows no boundaries and equality reigns supreme. With unwavering determination, they press onward, their hearts ablaze with the fervent hope of a brighter, more inclusive tomorrow. And as time unfolds, they've remained not just allies but close friends, their bond a testament to the enduring power of love and solidarity.

As Duke DeAndre and Prince Manvendra sat in their Mumbai home in Malad West, a cozy haven that held a special place in their hearts, the news of Duke DeAndre's canceled visa shattered the tranquility of their lives. This small flat, given to Prince Manvendra in 2008–09 to keep him from returning to the ancestral property in Santa Cruz West, held significance beyond its humble appearance. Situated across the street from Prince Manvendra's beloved music teacher, this location held a cherished connection to his past, making it the perfect choice for their abode.

For Duke DeAndre, this flat had been their sanctuary since 2014, the only residence that truly felt like their own, offering a sense of privacy and comfort amidst the bustling city of Mumbai. As they grappled with the impending departure, the weight of leaving behind their cherished haven bore down on them with a profound sense of loss.

Each corner of their Malad West home held echoes of their shared experiences and the journey they had embarked upon together. From the laughter that reverberated through its walls to the quiet moments of solace they found within its confines, this humble abode had been witness to the evolution of their love story.

As Prince Manvendra packed their belongings, memories flooded his mind, each item imbued with the warmth of nostalgia and the bittersweet tang of farewell. Leaving behind their cozy haven felt like bidding adieu to a piece of their souls, a tangible reminder of the life they had built together in the heart of Mumbai.

Walking out of their Malad West home for the last time, Prince Manvendra carried with him a myriad of emotions—sadness for the memories left behind, hope for the future that lay ahead, and an unshakeable gratitude for the love that had flourished within its walls.

Though they were forced to bid farewell to their beloved home, the bond they shared remained unyielding, a steadfast beacon guiding them through the uncertainties that lay ahead. In the face of adversity, their love served as a source of strength and resilience, illuminating the path forward with its unwavering glow.

Leaving behind their Malad West home marked the end of one chapter in their lives, but it also heralded the beginning of a new journey filled with endless possibilities. As they ventured forth into the unknown, hand in hand, they drew comfort from the knowledge that no matter where life took them, their love would always be their guiding light. And as time passed, they remained not just partners but soulmates, their bond strengthened by the wisdom and enduring power of love.

Living in India alongside his beloved husband, Prince Manvendra, immersed Duke DeAndre in the vibrant tapestry of Indian culture, where each day brought new experiences and connections. But when the relentless waves of the Covid-19 pandemic crashed upon their shores, their lives were swept into a whirlwind of uncertainty. The Indian government's decision to cancel Duke DeAndre's visa amid the pandemic, compounded by the lack of recognition of marriage equality, shattered their sense of stability and belonging.

The news of his impending departure from India weighed heavily on Duke DeAndre's heart, tearing him away from the life they had built together. Saying goodbye to their friends, their home in

Malad West—a cozy sanctuary that held the echoes of their shared laughter and dreams—was a heartbreaking ordeal. The realization that he would be separated from Prince Manvendra, his rock and anchor, filled him with an overwhelming sense of loss and despair.

Yet, amidst the turmoil, a glimmer of determination flickered within him. He refused to succumb to despair, drawing strength from the unwavering support of his husband and the resilience of the LGBTQIA+ community. With each passing day, he resolved to channel his energy into advocacy, determined to be a voice for those whose rights were silenced by discrimination and prejudice.

As Duke DeAndre embarked on the journey back to the United States, guided by the wisdom of love, he carried with him the enduring bond he shared with Prince Manvendra. Though physically separated from India, the bonds forged with its people remained etched in his heart, serving as a beacon of hope and solidarity in his darkest hours.

Through the trials and tribulations of his journey, Duke DeAndre gleaned invaluable lessons on the transformative power of love and resilience. Each obstacle became a testament to the indomitable strength that resides within, propelling him forward with a renewed sense of purpose. As he navigated the complexities of his new reality, guided by the wisdom of love, he remained steadfast in his commitment to fostering understanding and acceptance, bridging the gap between cultures, and advocating for equality with unwavering resolve. And despite the physical distance, he and Prince Manvendra remained connected, their bond a testament to the enduring strength of love across borders.

"Prince Manvendra and Duke DeAndre served as the guests of honor at Mauritius Pride 2017."

"Due to security threats, Prince Manvendra and Duke DeAndre were accompanied by a team of highly qualified security personnel at all times while out in public during the Pride event in Mauritius."

"Prince Manvendra and Duke DeAndre served as the grand marshals of the Mauritius Pride march. During the event, a group of extremists pushed through security, but the police and security team quickly regained control of the situation."

"Prince Manvendra and Duke DeAndre attending the Hong Kong Pride Parade 2018 to protest the #FreeMyLibrary campaign. The march took place on Saturday, November 18, moving from Causeway Bay to Central."

'Prince Manvendra and Duke DeAndre meeting with leadership from the LGBTQIA+ organization, including Laxmi Narayan Tripathi and Sonal Giani."

Broadway to Bombay Event in Vadodara, Gujarat at Alliance Française: Prince Manvendra and Duke DeAndre Touring with the "Broadway to Bombay: Unleashing the Emotions You Cannot Express" Tour

"Prince Manvendra and Duke DeAndre meeting with Violet Chachki, a renowned drag figure, and Dr. Samarpan Maiti, Mr. Gay India 2017, in Mumbai."

"Prince Manvendra and Duke DeAndre with Cathy Renna at the Human Rights Conference: World Pride 2019."

"Prince Manvendra and Jessica Stern participating in a panel discussion at the Human Rights Conference in New York."

"From left to right: Duke DeAndre, Prince Manvendra, Mrs. Lola Finkelstein, and Carla Fine. Carla Fine, one of the hosts of the fundraiser for the LGBTQIA+ community campus ashram in Rajpipla, honors her sister Janet Fine with the Janet Fine Cottage."

"So nice to see these faces at the fundraiser for the LGBTQIA+ Community Campus ashram Rajpipla, in NYC during World Pride. Left to right in the background: Nawab Kazim Ali Khan, Bess Hepworth, Amao Leota Lu, Trish Moran, James Murry."

"Prince Manvendra and Duke DeAndre receiving a gift of Jackie Evancho's CD. Also in the photo are Michael Evancho and Rachel Evancho, at the fundraiser in NYC during World Pride."

"Left to right: Dolores Catania, American television personality; Achilles Emmanuel; Duke DeAndre; Prince Manvendra at the fundraiser in Chelsea, NY for the LGBTQIA+ Community Campus Ashram, Rajpipla, India."

"From left to right: Adam Pasha, Duke DeAndre, and Prince Manvendra at the LGBTQIA+ Community Campus Ashram in Rajpipla."

"Prince Manvendra and Duke DeAndre ready to attend the 74th Independence Day of India on August 15, 2020. The celebration took place amidst the global pandemic, with face masks required in public settings."

PART 4

THE CONTINUING JOURNEY (2021-2023)

9

Reflection on Ten Years

As Duke DeAndre, life had always seemed to cater to his every whim and fancy, enveloping him in a cocoon of luxury and privilege. Yet, when the pandemic's shadow descended, it stripped away the facade of opulence, leaving him adrift in the unfamiliar landscape of South Florida. The once-familiar trappings of comfort vanished, replaced by the harsh reality of joblessness and isolation.

Faced with the daunting prospect of survival, he assumed a new guise as "J. R.," plunging into the anonymity of menial work at a local fast-food joint. Scrubbing dishes and toiling behind the scenes became his new reality, a stark departure from the world of extravagance he had grown accustomed to. Concealing his true identity became second nature, a necessary sacrifice in his quest for stability.

The weight of separation from his beloved husband, Prince Manvendra, bore down heavily upon him, the ache of longing echoing in every beat of his heart. Yet, in the depths of adversity, he discovered an inner resilience he never knew existed. Each day became a battle against despair, every dish washed a testament to his unwavering resolve.

Despite the physical and emotional toll, he persevered, clinging to the belief that better days lay ahead. In the midst of uncertainty, a glimmer of hope emerged through H1927 LLC, a venture aimed at providing aid to the LGBTQIA+ community in India. Though his efforts were met with roadblocks, the spirit of resilience burned bright within him, refusing to be extinguished by setbacks.

In the midst of adversity, Duke DeAndre found himself deeply connected to higher spiritual energy and the soothing power of crystals. Guided by an inner resonance with the universe, he discovered solace in the embrace of divine forces. A picture of the royal family goddess, Harsiddhi Mataji, accompanied Duke DeAndre, serving as a symbol of divine protection and guidance during turbulent times.

Amidst the darkest nights, Duke DeAndre drew strength from his spiritual practices and the energy of the crystals that surrounded him. Through meditation and introspection, he tapped into a reservoir of inner peace and resilience, allowing him to navigate the challenges with grace and fortitude. In moments of doubt and despair, the unwavering bond between Prince Manvendra and him served as a beacon of light, illuminating the path forward with love and hope. Their connection transcended physical distance, weaving a sacred thread of love and resilience that bound them together, even in the face of adversity.

Through the trials and tribulations of his journey in South Florida, Duke DeAndre learned that love is not merely a fleeting emotion but a steadfast anchor in tumultuous seas. It is the driving force that propels them forward, infusing even the bleakest moments with hope and purpose. And though the road ahead may be fraught with challenges, he takes solace in the knowledge that with love as his compass, he can weather any storm.

As of October 2020, Duke DeAndre found himself in the United States, while Prince Manvendra continued to navigate the intricate balance between his responsibilities as chairman of Lakshya Trust and his personal endeavors. Leading Lakshya Trust demanded Prince Manvendra's unwavering commitment as he oversaw its operations and establishments, often shuttling between Mumbai and Rajpipla. Behind the scenes, there were countless moments of decision-making and coordination, ensuring that protocols were maintained, and initiatives were aligned with the mission, guided by the wisdom of love.

In 2021, amidst his ongoing commitments, Prince Manvendra was honored to be appointed as a host by Red FM Radio for a podcast dedicated exclusively to LGBTQIA+ issues, titled *LGBT Kyun...All questions answered*. This opportunity allowed him to amplify marginalized voices and provide a platform for meaningful conversations about LGBTQIA+ rights and inclusion. Behind the scenes, there were hours of preparation and planning as Prince Manvendra delved into topics ranging from activism to personal stories of resilience, fueled by the wisdom of love.

Prince Manvendra's involvement with Eyes Open International, an American nonprofit organization combating human trafficking, marked a significant milestone in his advocacy journey. Joining their advisory board in 2021 provided him with a platform to contribute to the fight against modern-day slavery and exploitation. Behind the scenes, there were discussions and strategizing sessions aimed at maximizing impact and advancing the mission of liberation and empowerment, all guided by the wisdom of love. In a special episode of his podcast, Prince Manvendra interviewed Harold D'Souza, the founder of Eyes Open International, focusing on human trafficking and exploring how the LGBTQIA+ community can effectively combat this issue.

The Covid-19 pandemic cast a long shadow over their lives, ushering in uncertainty and upheaval on a global scale. Amidst the chaos, the development of the vaccine emerged as a ray of hope, promising a pathway to normalcy. For Duke DeAndre, it also brought a glimmer of opportunity in the midst of adversity.

In the wake of the pandemic's economic fallout, finding employment became an uphill battle. Despite Duke DeAndre's expertise as a makeup artist and skincare professional, job prospects dwindled as businesses shuttered their doors. However, the arrival of the vaccine signaled a turning point, igniting a newfound sense of optimism within him.

With determination driven by newfound hope, Duke DeAndre wasted no time in securing his vaccination appointment, recognizing it as a crucial step towards reviving his career. As the vaccine surged through his veins, so too did a renewed sense of purpose and possibility.

In the wake of his vaccination, doors began to open, leading Duke DeAndre to a coveted position at Bloomingdale's in the Town Center at Boca Raton. Despite the lengthy commute, the opportunity to work with Space NK, a renowned beauty retailer, filled him with excitement and determination.

Stepping into the elegant confines of Bloomingdale's, he felt a sense of belonging amidst the polished displays and chic ambiance. Each day presented a fresh canvas upon which to showcase his skills, and he embraced the challenge with unwavering dedication.

Despite the trials and tribulations, the wisdom of love sustained Duke DeAndre through the storm. It reminded him that even in the face of adversity, there are opportunities for growth and renewal. And as he navigated through the challenges, he emerged not only resilient but also grateful for the chance to rebuild and thrive in the wake of the pandemic.

10

Beyond the Decade

In April 2022, Prince Manvendra found himself standing amidst a symphony of applause, deeply humbled to receive the World Peace Ambassador Award from the Asian-African Chamber of Commerce and Industry. The hall reverberated with the significance of the moment, each echo a poignant reminder of the interconnectedness of the global community. As the award gleamed in his hands, Prince Manvendra's heart swelled with gratitude, recognizing the responsibility it bestowed upon him to foster peace and understanding across borders. Behind the scenes, amidst the glitz and glamor, there were moments of quiet reflection. In the sanctuary of his thoughts, Prince Manvendra contemplated the weight of this honor, reaffirming his unwavering commitment to promoting harmony and unity, guided by the wisdom of love.

But amidst the accolades and recognition, Prince Manvendra's heart remained anchored to the ground-breaking vision taking shape under his watchful gaze. During this time, he immersed himself in overseeing the Royal Establishment Hanumanteshwar and the LGBTQIA+ community campus ashram affectionately known as QueerBagh. From the labyrinthine interiors of the buildings, where every tile and brushstroke held the promise of inclusivity, to the meticulous planning of gardens and walkways, every detail was infused with the wisdom of love. Here, amidst the whirr of construction and the scent of fresh paint, Prince Manvendra and Duke DeAndre's shared dreams breathed life into the campus. They envisioned a sanctuary where love knew no bounds, where every brick and beam whispered tales of acceptance and belonging. And as they tirelessly worked to manifest their vision, the waterproofing of the terrace became more than just a practical task—it marked another triumphant step forward in their journey toward realizing their collective dream.

Yet, amid the flurry of activity, Prince Manvendra's heart remained tethered to the memories of resilience and determination that paved his path. Being honored with the Gujarat Gaurav Award by the Ahmedabad Management Association on Gujarat Day, May 1st, 2022, held a special significance for him. As he stood on stage, basking in the glow of admiration, Prince Manvendra couldn't help but be transported back in time. Each applause was a reverberation of the challenges overcome, the victories celebrated, and the countless lives touched by their collective efforts. Behind the curtain of his composure, there lay a tapestry of memories woven with threads of resilience and determination, each strand fueling his resolve to continue striving for progress and positive change in the world.

As Prince Manvendra and Duke DeAndre delve into the beginnings of their memoir, they are overwhelmed with gratitude and introspection. One pivotal moment etched in their memories is the invitation they received in May 2022 to attend the esteemed Amaranter Ball at the Grand Hotel in Stockholm, Sweden. This historic event, tracing back to Queen Christina's initiation in 1683, has been a beacon of tradition and camaraderie for centuries, hosting dignitaries from royal families worldwide, including HSH Princess Marie-Louise zu Sayn Wittgenstein-Berleburg. To be among such esteemed guests was profoundly humbling.

The ceremony took on a deeper significance as Count Fredrik Taube, the General Grand Master of the Great Order of Amarant, bestowed upon them the Knight of the Fourth Order, Chevalier Degree, the Vigilant. This esteemed honor, symbolized by a distinctive badge elegantly draped over the right shoulder to the left hip on a white ribbon with blue edges, is a testament to their unwavering vigilance in advocacy and contributions to societal advancement.

Surrounded by cherished friends who had journeyed far and wide, the occasion was imbued with love and support that has sustained them throughout their journey. Their presence reaffirmed their bonds and filled them with profound gratitude.

The conferral of the Fourth Chevalier Degree marks a significant milestone, recognizing their global advocacy for LGBTQIA+ intersectionality and commitment to societal progress. As proud members of both the Great Order and the International Arcadia Chapter, they pledge to uphold the cherished values of these esteemed organizations, perpetuating a legacy of inclusivity and cultural enrichment.

Their resolve to foster a more inclusive world remains steadfast. The induction into the Fourth Chevalier Degree serves as a poignant reminder of their duty to champion positive change and uphold the principles of equality and justice. Guided by the wisdom of love, they are emboldened to continue their endeavors with unwavering dedication, ensuring that their actions resonate with compassion and progress for generations to come.

Arriving in Stockholm, the first evening at the Story Hotel set the stage for the enchanting weekend ahead. Amidst an intriguing mix of creative minds, they attended the soft launch of Michael Lee Jackson's photo book, *Super Bloom*. The event introduced them to a diverse array of individuals, each contributing their unique spirit to the gathering.

On day two, they ventured into Scandinavia's Viking past at Stockholm's Viking Museum in Djurgårdsvägen for a sit-down dinner. The Amaranters, eager to immerse themselves in the festivities, donned costumes, transforming into Norsemen and women for the night. The evening commenced with an immersive journey through Norse mythology in the museum's basement, setting a whimsical tone.

The dinner, curated by Matthew—a vegan for thirty years—featured an all-Viking, plant-based feast, minimizing the event's environmental impact. Drinking mead amidst tenth-century Swedish artifacts was a captivating experience, evoking the legendary Viking era.

The magic peaked when long-term Amaranters Patrick Martin and Vanessa Sterling renewed their vows outside the museum, orchestrated as a surprise for both the couple and guests. Dressed in traditional Icelandic attire, the exchange of vows amidst the ambiance of ancient relics was a truly enchanting moment.

The conferral of the Fourth Chevalier Degree was a testament to their unwavering vigilance in advocacy and contributions to societal advancement, a recognition that filled them with profound gratitude and a renewed sense of purpose. Guided by the wisdom of love, they were emboldened to continue their endeavors with unwavering dedication, ensuring that their actions resonated with compassion and progress for generations to come.

In the lush embrace of May 2022, Prince Manvendra embarked on a soul-stirring journey across New Jersey, where every step unveiled a tapestry woven with poignant moments and heartfelt connections. It all began with a warm embrace from Kris and John Lamb, whose open-hearted hospitality enveloped him in a cocoon of music and laughter. In their home, Prince Manvendra found himself immersed in the vibrant rhythm of their lives, cherishing each shared moment with the Lamb family and their circle of friends.

One unforgettable stop on this odyssey was Ethos Organic Farm in Long Valley, a verdant sanctuary where Dr. Ron Weiss and farm manager Nora Pugliese served as guides through nature's bounty. Over a delectable breakfast crafted by Asha Gala, the Primary Care Director, they savored the earth's treasures and exchanged tales of resilience and hope.

At Duke Farms in Hillsborough, Prince Manvendra was led on an enchanting tour by Von, a trans-man whose spirit resonated deeply with their shared journey of love and acceptance. Against the backdrop of rolling fields, Prince Manvendra's harmonium melodies intertwined with the gentle breeze, painting the air with a symphony of unity.

Beyond the Decade

The journey took on a deeper resonance as rehearsals commenced for the Open Heart Concerts tour, a tribute to Kris Lamb's brother, Bud Oddsen. Infused with Bud's memory, each note composed in collaboration with Mark Miller carried messages of inclusion and love, resonating with heartfelt intention.

The tour crescendoed with a series of unforgettable events, from film screenings to concerts and talks. At Our Lady of Sorrows Church in South Orange, Prince Manvendra shared his music, casting ripples of love across a captivated audience. Meanwhile, the *Pieces of Us* documentary screening in Morristown ignited conversations about resilience, knitting their community closer together.

The climax awaited at the Harmonium Choral Society Dinner, where Prince Manvendra stood amidst esteemed musicians and supporters, sharing his advocacy work and musical gift. In that moment, enveloped by a wave of gratitude, he realized the transformative power of art in inspiring change.

As the tour drew to a close, Prince Manvendra reflected on their journey, from the verdant landscapes of Earth Care Farm in Rhode Island to the serene shores of Block Island. Each moment, saturated with love and connection, forged bonds that transcended boundaries, uniting them in a shared mission of spreading love and acceptance.

In June 2022, the journey took a poignant turn as Prince Manvendra made a special stop in Bedford, New York. Hosted by new friends Andy and Evan, he found solace in their hospitality, surrounded by the warmth of their newly renovated guesthouse. Despite Martha Stewart's absence, her gesture of fresh farm eggs added to the enchantment of breakfast, shared amidst laughter and camaraderie.

Further connections were forged at the Glen Arbor Golf Club, where Prince Manvendra met audience members from the film screening. Yet, the pinnacle of his time in Bedford was the unexpected party thrown in his honor by Andy and Evan, a gathering of creative souls that left an indelible mark on his heart. In those fleeting moments, the wisdom of love illuminated their path, guiding them to embrace each encounter with open hearts and minds, igniting sparks of change along the way.

During their time in India, the lives of Prince Manvendra and Duke DeAndre intertwined with that of Kevin Stea, a luminary in the world of dance and entertainment. Kevin's illustrious career, peppered with collaborations with iconic figures like Madonna and Michael Jackson, brought an air of creativity and excitement to their friendship. Welcomed into his Hollywood Hills abode during their visits to the Los Angeles area, they shared unforgettable moments, forging lasting bonds.

One particular memory stood out vividly, etched in the fabric of their shared experiences. It was during their visit to Fort Lauderdale when Kevin orchestrated a special treat: an invitation to the VIP Taco Bell Drag Brunch at Beach Place on June 26th. As the mastermind behind the tour's choreography, Kevin ensured each performance left an indelible mark on its audience. Little did they realize that this brunch would mark the culmination of their journey together.

In the midst of the excitement, a serendipitous encounter unfolded. Duke DeAndre, once known as "J. R." from his days toiling in a fast-food restaurant during the pandemic, spotted his former manager, Rose, among the bustling crowd. In a moment of spontaneity and guided by the wisdom of love, he revealed his true identity as a prince and his marriage to Prince Manvendra.

To their surprise and delight, Rose welcomed Duke DeAndre with open arms, reminiscing about his dedication and hard work. It was a heartwarming reminder of the bonds formed in the most unexpected of places and the power of authenticity.

Joined by their dear friend Maxwell, the four of them entered the event, greeted by a dazzling array of performances by local drag queens in celebration of Pride Month. With names like Jellika Boom, D'Vice Dion, and Jah'Syra, the atmosphere was electric, pulsating with the vibrant energy of self-expression and acceptance.

Surrounded by love, laughter, and acceptance, they reveled in the joyous celebration of Pride and the kaleidoscope of diversity within the LGBTQIA+ community. At that moment, as they basked in the warmth of friendship and camaraderie, they were reminded once again of the unwavering support of their loved ones and the beauty of embracing their true selves.

Their journey to Ohio, orchestrated by their tireless advocate friend Harold D'Souza, was akin to stepping into a realm of new insights and profound experiences. Coinciding with Ohio's vibrant 4th of July celebration, Red, White & Blue Ash, allowed them to tour Cincinnati Works, an organization dedicated to empowering individuals to achieve independence. Meeting with Mayor Aftab Pureval enriched their experience, learning about his journey as the city's first Asian American mayor.

As they ventured from meetings at the Statehouse in Columbus to a solemn vow renewal ceremony at the historic Abraham Pillar, each moment seemed to radiate with significance, urging them to confront injustice head-on. The weight of their voices reverberated in the corridors of power and echoed through the hallowed grounds of historic landmarks, reminding them of the importance of advocacy in the face of adversity. Interactions with local activists and community leaders in Ohio became a testament to the transformative power of solidarity, as they witnessed firsthand the unwavering commitment to the fight for LGBTQIA+ rights. Each encounter fueled their determination, reaffirming their resolve to be agents of change in the ongoing battle for equality and justice.

Surrounded by cherished friends and family, including Kris and John Lamb, the renewal of their vows on their ninth wedding anniversary became a powerful statement against the lack of recognition for same-sex marriages. A documentary team captured every emotion, immersing them in a profoundly meaningful occasion. Their reaffirmed commitment to each other was further celebrated at Stonewall Columbus. Surrounded by loved ones, the occasion was filled with love and joy. The unexpected arrival of their dear friend Tiffany Otto, whom they had met in the Amaranter Society, added an extra layer of warmth and meaning to the celebration. Moreover, the surprise Bollywood dance by Thiago Amaral from Brazil added to the day's joy and camaraderie, making it a truly unforgettable experience filled with love, friendship, and beautiful surprises.

In Cleveland, meaningful interactions, including lunch meetings with members of the Collaborative to End Human Trafficking and a public forum at the LGBTQIA+ Center, left a lasting impression. The warmth and hospitality extended to them by the community, including their dear friend Dr. Swagata Banik, made their visit even more memorable.

Their involvement with Eyes Open International went beyond activism; it was a deeply personal mission guided by the wisdom of love—the belief that compassion, empathy, and solidarity are potent weapons against injustice.

Reflecting on their journey, they were grateful for the opportunity to share their message of hope and resilience with others. Moving forward, their commitment to amplifying marginalized voices and fostering a more inclusive society remained resolute. Together, they would continue to shine a light on the hidden scourge of human trafficking, keeping their eyes open to the suffering of others and working tirelessly to create a brighter, more equitable future for all.

On August 8th, 2022, Duke DeAndre's cycling adventure took an unexpected turn, as a sudden knee injury halted his journey and reshaped his reality. Despite exhaustive attempts to address it, the injury persisted, stripping away the activities that once defined his days with boundless joy and freedom. It was a profound shift, forcing him to confront newfound physical limitations and a redefined sense of self.

By August 13th, the injury had taken its toll, confining Duke DeAndre to a wheelchair during a weekend of filming in Orlando, Florida. However, Prince Manvendra, undeterred by his husband's physical discomfort, stepped in with unwavering support. Amidst the demands of engaging with LGBTQIA+ leadership and participating in documentary filming, Prince Manvendra ensured Duke DeAndre's well-being. From arranging doctor visits to providing ice packs and keeping his partner's leg elevated in a comfortable position during filming, Prince Manvendra's care was a testament to the wisdom of love guiding them through adversity.

In the midst of these challenges, solace awaited at Unity of Central Florida, where Duke DeAndre and Prince Manvendra found refuge in the nurturing embrace of the congregation. Here, amidst cherished friends, they celebrated their ninth anniversary with a poignant Celebration of Love ceremony, renewing their bond amidst expressions of gratitude and the unwavering support of their community.

Their time in Orlando also offered a culinary journey at Chef Art Smith's Homecomin'. Though Chef Art Smith was unable to join them personally, Prince Manvendra ensured that every moment was savored, despite the absence of the master chef. With attention to detail and unwavering hospitality, the experience was a testament to the enduring bonds forged through shared moments of warmth and connection.

As they reflected on these experiences, Duke DeAndre and Prince Manvendra found solace in the profound impact of love, resilience, and community. Their journey stood as a testament to the transformative power of these values, guiding them through life's twists and turns with grace and fortitude.

As the tragic events of June 12th, 2016, unfolded, Prince Manvendra and Duke DeAndre had found themselves deeply impacted by the shooting at the Pulse nightclub, a beloved gay club in Orlando. Forty-nine people were murdered, and fifty-three others wounded on that terrible night.

Fast forward to August 2022, during filming with Reverend Terri Steed Pierce, the senior pastor at Joy Metropolitan Community Church, memories of that devastating day resurfaced, casting a shadow over their conversation. Reverend Pierce's words carried the weight of lived experience and unwavering commitment to her community. She recounted the heartbreak she felt in the aftermath of the massacre, a day that forever altered the fabric of their lives and served as a stark reminder of the fragility of life in the face of hate.

Their meeting with Reverend Pierce took place immediately after visiting the Pulse memorial wall. The heart-shaped stained glass light catcher, a poignant gift from Orlando Commissioner Patty Sheehan, served as a tangible reminder of the lives lost and the wounds that still lingered in the hearts of many. At that moment, amidst profound grief and resilience, Reverend Pierce shared her recent experiences at the local cemetery, preparing for the funerals of the victims. Her solemn task underscored the depth of her compassion and dedication, from finding a sun-drenched corner large enough for all forty-nine individuals to organizing a human chain to shield mourners from the hateful protests of groups like the Westboro Baptist Church.

Reflecting on the tragic events of June 12th, 2016, Prince Manvendra and Duke DeAndre vividly recalled waking up in Los Angeles to the devastating news of the Pulse nightclub shooting. The weight of the tragedy hung heavy as they prepared to participate in the LA Gay Pride Parade. Heightened security measures had underscored the somber reality of the world they lived in, where acts of violence against the LGBTQIA+ community continued to threaten their sense of safety and belonging.

Yet, amidst the grief and uncertainty, there remained a glimmer of hope—a belief in the transformative power of love. As they navigated the complexities of their world, it was love that guided them forward, inspiring them to stand in solidarity with one another and strive for a brighter, more inclusive future.

In the face of adversity, they were reminded that it is through acts of compassion, empathy, and understanding that they could truly make a difference. With the wisdom of love as their compass, Prince Manvendra and Duke DeAndre remained steadfast in their commitment to building a world where all individuals are valued, respected, and embraced for who they are.

As Prince Manvendra and Duke DeAndre ventured into Orlando during their visit, a solemn pilgrimage to the Pulse memorial wall awaited them, a site steeped in a multitude of emotions. The atmosphere enveloped them in a blend of fear, love, grace, and hope, stirring memories of the tragic events that unfolded on June 12th, 2016.

Standing before the memorial, they were confronted with the weight of the tragedy that had befallen the LGBTQIA+ community and the world at large. Pulse, once a vibrant gathering place for joy and acceptance, had become a symbol of unspeakable loss and grief. The magnitude of the event reverberated across the globe, serving as a stark reminder of the pervasive impact of hate and intolerance.

The planned National Pulse Memorial and Museum, intended to honor the victims and preserve their memory, stood as a testament to the resilience of the human spirit in the face of tragedy. However, their hearts sank as they learned that the plans for the memorial had been permanently suspended, leaving a void in the collective effort to commemorate the lives lost.

Amidst the sorrow and reflection, the wisdom of love whispered to them, reminding them of the enduring power of compassion and unity in the face of adversity. Each message left behind by visitors at the site became a poignant testament to the human capacity for resilience and solidarity.

A message from the onePULSE Foundation encapsulated the spirit of resilience and unity that emerged in the aftermath of the tragedy. It reminded them that the victims hailed from diverse backgrounds, representing a tapestry of humanity united by a shared quest for love, acceptance, and belonging.

Walking through the interim memorial, they felt compelled to add their voices to the chorus of hope and remembrance. Each message became a pledge to honor the memory of the fallen and to stand against hatred and bigotry. Though the journey toward healing and reconciliation may be fraught with challenges, the resilience and solidarity displayed by the community serve as a beacon of hope for the future.

In the shadow of tragedy, the wisdom of love reminded them of the fragility of life and the importance of cherishing every moment with loved ones. The Pulse memorial wall became not only a place of remembrance but also a catalyst for introspection and renewal, inspiring them to continue their advocacy for love, acceptance, and equality for all.

As Prince Manvendra prepared for his journey back to India, the weight of duty as the Crown Prince of Rajpipla beckoned him home, particularly to the revered Goddess Harsiddhi Mataji temple. Nestled in the heart of Rajpipla, Gujarat, this sacred sanctuary held profound historical and spiritual significance, attracting pilgrims far and wide, especially during the vibrant Navratri festival. Despite the solemnity of his departure, the bond forged by the wisdom of love with Duke DeAndre sustained him as he braced himself for the separation ahead.

Saying goodbye to Duke DeAndre was an emotionally taxing ordeal for Prince Manvendra, compounded by the ongoing treatments for Duke DeAndre's knee injury and the arduous physical therapy sessions. Yet, buoyed by the enduring strength of their love, they faced their farewells with a mixture of fortitude and tenderness. As Prince Manvendra embarked on his journey homeward, the echo of Duke DeAndre's unwavering support resonated within him, reassuring him in the face of the impending distance between them.

The prospect of parting ways was undeniably daunting, but the wisdom of love served as their guiding light, illuminating the path forward with resilience and hope. Despite the geographical chasm that would momentarily separate them, the threads of their affection remained steadfast, intertwining their hearts across continents and time zones.

As Prince Manvendra returned to fulfill his duties in Rajpipla, his thoughts often drifted back to Duke DeAndre, his well-being a constant presence in his mind and heart. Yet, amidst the obligations of royalty, he found solace in knowing that Duke DeAndre was embarking on a new chapter of his own, navigating a promising career trajectory with American Express. The flexibility afforded by his new role, allowing him to work from home and prioritize his health, offered a glimmer of reassurance amid the uncertainties of their temporary separation.

Though miles apart, their connection remained unyielding, anchored by the enduring bond of love and mutual support. Each passing day brought them closer to the moment when they would reunite, their shared journey infused with the unwavering promise of love's enduring embrace.

Cathy Renna extended an invitation to Duke DeAndre to attend the National LGBTQ Taskforce gala in Miami Beach, Florida, on October 22nd, 2022. This would mark Duke DeAndre's final public appearance for some time.

As the date of the gala approached, Duke DeAndre eagerly prepared for what promised to be an evening of celebration, solidarity, and profound connections. Every detail, from selecting the perfect attire to rehearsing his walk with a cane, was meticulously curated with the utmost care and attention.

The night of the gala arrived, casting a shimmering glow over the balmy Miami Beach skyline. The venue, a palatial ballroom adorned with opulent chandeliers and cascading floral arrangements, exuded an aura of grandeur and elegance. As Duke DeAndre and Cathy Renna stepped onto the red carpet, camera flashes flickered like stars in the night sky, capturing the essence of his presence with each dazzling moment.

Inside the gala, the air hummed with excitement and anticipation as guests mingled amidst the melodic strains of live music. The room was a tapestry of diversity, with attendees from all walks of life converging in a shared celebration of love and acceptance. Amidst the jubilant ambiance, Duke DeAndre found himself enveloped in a whirlwind of greetings and heartfelt conversations. Each interaction was a testament to the profound impact of his advocacy work and the enduring bonds forged within the LGBTQIA+ community.

As the evening unfolded, speeches were delivered with passion and conviction, echoing through the hallowed halls of the ballroom like rallying cries for progress and change. Duke DeAndre stood with grace and dignity as his name was announced as an honored attendee, his heart brimming with gratitude and hope for the future.

The gala reached its crescendo with a dazzling display of unity and solidarity, as guests joined hands in a symbolic gesture of support for the LGBTQIA+ community. Against the backdrop of a starlit sky, Duke DeAndre stood, his spirit lifted by the wisdom of love that guided him through this momentous evening.

As the night drew to a close, Duke DeAndre reflected on the profound significance of the evening. It was not merely a gala but a testament to the resilience, courage, and unwavering spirit of the LGBTQIA+ community—a beacon of hope lighting the way towards a brighter, more inclusive tomorrow.

11

Forever Royal

Duke DeAndre's health had deteriorated over the last four months, and he was now using a wheelchair. He sought medical advice following the guidance he had received in the meditation session, found a doctor, and received a diagnosis of spondyloarthritis, a condition characterized by inflammation in the spine and joints. Despite the initial shock, Prince Manvendra and Duke DeAndre leaned into the wisdom of love, drawing strength from their shared belief that together, they could navigate any obstacle.

In May 2023, Duke DeAndre made the courageous decision to prioritize his health and stepped away from his role at American Express. However, this shift in trajectory did not dampen his spirits or extinguish his passions. Guided by the wisdom of love, he embarked on a transformative journey, reshaping his company, H1927 LLC, into a vibrant e-commerce business, publishing house, and DEI agency.

Despite the physical limitations imposed by his health condition, Duke DeAndre remained resolute in his determination, refusing to let adversity define his aspirations. Through unwavering perseverance and the boundless power of love, he demonstrated that with faith and determination, any challenge can be conquered, and any dream can be realized.

When Prince Manvendra received the email from Duke DeAndre about his diagnosis of spondyloarthritis, he was hosting a group of foreign gay travelers at the Royal Establishment Hanumanteshwar. They had stopped by for a day-long outing at the LGBTQIA+ community campus ashram. As Prince Manvendra absorbed the news, emotions overwhelmed him, and he found himself alone, shedding tears as a flood of feelings surged forth. With a racing mind, he grappled with what steps to take next. Despite the weight of the situation, he knew he had to compose himself and attend to their guests. Yet, an underlying sense of concern lingered, clinging to him like an invisible cloak.

Drawing upon the wisdom of love, Prince Manvendra embarked on a journey to seek guidance from medical professionals and healers across India. Among them was their esteemed friend, Guruwarya Hazrat Abdulbhai Babaji, whom they consulted extensively. Through WhatsApp, Guruwarya Hazrat Abdulbhai Babaji reached out to Duke DeAndre, offering valuable time for consultation and imparting a beautiful mantra to aid in Duke DeAndre's evening meditations, facilitating an energetic shift within the body.

In this quest for answers, Prince Manvendra left no stone unturned, exploring a myriad of approaches ranging from Western medical advice to spiritual counsel, and even delving into Ayurveda, the ancient natural system of medicine originating in India over 3000 years ago. Derived from the Sanskrit words *ayur* (life) and *veda* (science or knowledge), Ayurveda translates to the "knowledge of life."

Through this comprehensive exploration, Prince Manvendra sought to uncover the best path forward for Duke DeAndre, blending ancient wisdom with modern expertise to navigate the challenges ahead with courage and resilience.

Duke DeAndre's experience with spondyloarthritis had been a journey filled with challenges and resilience. Living with this condition, characterized by inflammation in the spine and joints, had fundamentally altered his daily life. Diagnosed with the HLA-B27 gene, he grappled with severe brain fog and fatigue, which had become constant companions in navigating through each day.

Living with a hidden disability like spondyloarthritis presented unique hurdles that were often misunderstood by others. It was a journey marked by invisible battles, where the weight of chronic pain and cognitive symptoms could be overwhelming. Despite the difficulty, he learned to lean into the wisdom of love, finding strength in the support of Prince Manvendra and their shared journey.

Adjusting to living with spondyloarthritis required significant changes in various aspects of his life. From adapting work responsibilities to reimagining leisure activities, every decision was influenced by the impact of this condition. While the road was challenging, he came to understand that with the right coping strategies and a consistent treatment plan, it was possible to live a fulfilling life despite the limitations imposed by spondyloarthritis.

The cognitive symptoms, often referred to as "brain fog," had been particularly challenging to navigate. Forgetfulness, dissociation, and difficulty with decision-making were constant companions, adding an extra layer of complexity to daily tasks. Despite these challenges, he found ways to cope and adapt, drawing strength from the resilience of individuals living with similar conditions.

Fatigue, another prevalent symptom of spondyloarthritis, had been a constant presence in his life. Unlike ordinary tiredness, fatigue persisted even after rest, impacting his energy levels and overall well-being. Recognizing the importance of managing this fatigue effectively had been crucial in maintaining a sense of balance and quality of life.

Through it all, the wisdom of love had been his guiding light, illuminating the path forward in the face of uncertainty. With the unwavering support of Prince Manvendra and the lessons learned from navigating the challenges of spondyloarthritis, Duke DeAndre continued to embrace each day with resilience and determination.

Duke DeAndre and Prince Manvendra have been deeply involved in the ongoing struggle for LGBTQIA+ rights and marriage equality in India. Over the years, they have witnessed both victories and setbacks. While courts in various states have taken steps towards recognizing the rights of same-sex couples, the protections offered have often been limited, providing only minimal benefits such as inheritance rights or police protection from family interference.

On November 14th, 2022, two same-sex couples filed writ petitions in the Supreme Court seeking legal recognition of same-sex marriages in India. They challenged the constitutionality of the Special Marriage Act of 1954, which restricts marriage to a 'male' and a 'female,' thus denying same-sex couples access to matrimonial benefits like adoption, surrogacy, and employment benefits. This sparked a series of legal actions, with similar petitions being considered by the Delhi and Kerala high courts.

Advocates successfully urged the consolidation of these petitions in the Supreme Court, leading to a five-judge Constitution Bench led by the Chief Justice of India, D. Y. Chandrachud. After hearings, the Bench reserved judgment, and on October 17th, 2023, delivered a landmark verdict. It ruled unanimously that LGBTQIA+ individuals do not have a fundamental right to marry under the Special Marriage Act, leaving the decision on recognizing non-heterosexual unions to Parliament and the state governments.

Reflecting on this legal battle, Duke DeAndre and Prince Manvendra emphasize the importance of the wisdom of love. They encourage advocacy for LGBTQIA+ rights and urge everyone to engage in dialogue and amplify their voices. Through unity, perseverance, and the unwavering pursuit of justice, they believe meaningful change can be achieved, leading to a society where love transcends boundaries.

"Prince Manvendra and Duke DeAndre at Mumbai International Airport, after days of packing up their home. The emotional stress of being separated during the global pandemic is evident. This is their last picture together in India, October 2020."

"Prince Manvendra and Duke DeAndre proudly hold a hand-carved limestone gift from Saint Von Lux and Frank Von Wortensee. This royal crest rendition has now become the symbol of H1927LLC, a beautiful testament to friendship and artistry."

"Arriving in South Florida, Duke DeAndre leans into his spiritual wisdom for guidance and strength. Engaging in meditation and manifestation, he focuses on the illuminated light of the Creator of All That Is to guide him through the darkness of life's circumstances."

"Group photo at the Amaranter Ball at the Grand Hotel in Stockholm, Sweden. This historic event, tracing back to Queen Christina's initiation in 1683, was where Count Fredrik Taube, General Grand Master of the Great Order of Amarant, bestowed upon Prince Manvendra and Duke DeAndre the Knight of the Fourth Order, Chevalier Degree, the Vigilant."

"From right to left: Mathew Devlen, HRH Prince Manvendra Singh Gohil of Rajpipla, HSH Princess Marie-Louise zu Sayn Wittgenstein-Berleburg, and HH Prince DeAndre, Duke of Hanumanteshwar, at the Amaranter Ball at the Grand Hotel in Stockholm, Sweden."

"From left to right: Alexander, Prince of Schaumburg-Lippe; HRH Crown Prince Manvendra Singh Gohil of Rajpipla; and HH Prince DeAndre, Duke of Hanumanteshwar, at the Amaranter Ball at the Grand Hotel in Stockholm, Sweden."

Mathew Devlen and the Esteemed Members of the International Arcadia Chapter 2024 in Stockholm, Sweden, Sending a Warm Hello to Prince Manvendra and Duke DeAndre

"Prince Manvendra and Kevin Stea at the VIP Taco Bell Drag Brunch at Beach Place in Fort Lauderdale, FL."

"Prince Manvendra and Duke DeAndre, captured right after Duke DeAndre revealed his true identity to Rose his former manager, as a prince and his marriage to Prince Manvendra, at the Drag Brunch in Fort Lauderdale, FL."

"Prince Manvendra and Duke DeAndre, joined by Tiffany Otto, whom they met at the Amaranter Society, celebrated their reaffirmation of commitment ceremony at Stonewall Columbus."

"At the Statehouse in Columbus, Ohio, meeting with Ohio Attorney General Dave Yost, alongside Harold D'Souza and Dancy D'Souza, before the solemn vow renewal ceremony at the historic Abraham Pillar."

"In a special episode of his podcast, Prince Manvendra interviews Harold D'Souza, founder of Eyes Open International, delving into human trafficking and exploring how the LGBTQIA+ community can play a vital role in combating this issue."

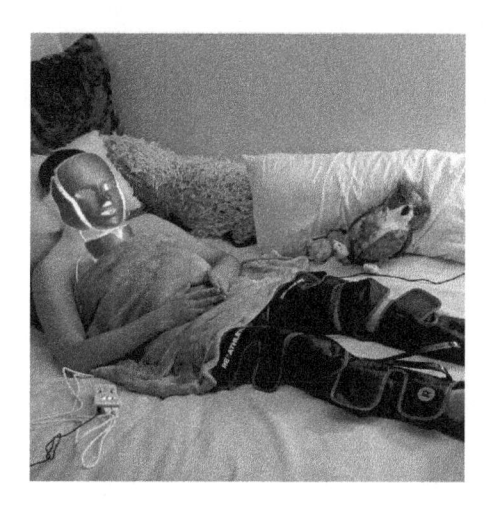

"Duke DeAndre explores various therapies for relief, from full leg and foot compression to light therapy and Transcutaneous Electrical Nerve Stimulation (TENS), seeking comfort and healing."

"Duke DeAndre using his wheelchair for support during a lively 4th of July celebration in the USA."

"Prince Manvendra and Duke DeAndre reunite in Mumbai, India, December 2023."

Afterword

As we pen down the final words of *A Royal Commitment: Ten Years of Marriage and Activism*, we find ourselves reflecting on the incredible journey we've shared with you, our readers. This epilogue serves as a glimpse into the aftermath of our story—a tale of love, resilience, and the enduring commitment to change.

Life, much like this memoir, is an ever-evolving narrative. The years have unfolded, and we've faced triumphs, challenges, and moments that have shaped the very fabric of our existence. Our commitment to love, activism, and inclusivity has not wavered; if anything, it has grown stronger with each passing day.

The world around us has also transformed. Progress has been made, conversations have shifted, and society is inching towards a more inclusive future. Yet, the journey is far from over. Our epilogue is not a conclusion but an acknowledgment that the quest for equality and understanding is ongoing.

In the years since the events recounted in these pages, we've continued our advocacy, stood at the forefront of conversations, and witnessed the impact of collective efforts to promote love and acceptance. The echoes of our story have reached beyond the boundaries of our personal experiences, resonating with individuals who seek inspiration, validation, or simply a connection.

We express our deepest gratitude to those who have embarked on this literary journey with us. Your support, understanding, and engagement have been invaluable. As we close this chapter, we invite you to carry forward the spirit of *A Royal Commitment* into your own lives.

Continue to challenge norms, foster understanding, and champion the causes that resonate with your heart. Love, in all its forms, has the power to transform lives and societies. Let it be a force that unites rather than divides, a beacon that guides us toward a more compassionate and accepting world.

In the end, this memoir is not just our story; it is a collective narrative of shared humanity. May it inspire conversations, provoke thoughts, and, above all, encourage a commitment to love that knows no bounds.

With heartfelt gratitude and a hopeful gaze toward the future,

> HRH Prince Manvendra Singh Gohil and HH Prince DeAndre, Duke of Hanumanteshwar

Acknowledgments

In the tapestry of our lives, woven with threads of love, commitment, and advocacy, numerous hands have played an integral role in shaping the narrative of *A Royal Commitment: Ten Years of Marriage and Activism*. This memoir is not just our story; it is a collective journey of support, resilience, and shared commitment to a world where love knows no bounds.

To our families, whose unwavering love and encouragement have been our anchor throughout this remarkable journey. Your acceptance and understanding have allowed us to navigate uncharted territories with courage and grace.

To our friends, allies, and chosen family—your support has been a constant source of strength. In moments of celebration and challenge, you have stood by us, reminding us that love is a shared experience.

To the LGBTQIA+ community, whose tireless advocacy and courage inspire us daily. Your collective resilience is the heartbeat of progress, and it fuels our commitment to a more inclusive world.

To the royal Gohil dynasty of Rajpipla, India, for embracing us with open hearts. Your acceptance is a testament to the power of love to transcend cultural boundaries and reshape traditions.

To the countless activists, pioneers, and individuals who have paved the way for LGBTQIA+ rights. Your legacy is the foundation upon which we stand, and we are indebted to your courage.

To the readers who embark on this journey with us, your willingness to explore the intersections of love and activism fuels our hope for a more compassionate and accepting world.

About the Authors

HRH Prince Manvendra Singh Gohil of Rajpipla:

As the 39th direct descendant of the Gohil dynasty in India, Prince Manvendra Singh Gohil stands at the intersection of tradition and progress. Born into royalty, he has not only embraced his heritage but has also become a trailblazer for LGBTQIA+ rights. An openly gay man, Prince Manvendra has dedicated his life to advocacy, founding the Lakshya Trust and the queer community campus ashram in Rajpipla. Renowned as a public speaker, he has delivered TED Talks, served as a keynote speaker for Corporate DEI events, spoken at NGLCC conferences, addressed audiences at universities worldwide, and participated as a keynote speaker in the UN Human Rights Conference. Additionally, Prince Manvendra has shared his insights as a guest teacher at Law University. His unwavering commitment continues to navigate the complexities of his royal lineage while championing inclusivity and love.

HH Prince DeAndre, Duke of Hanumanteshwar:

Duke DeAndre brings a unique and dynamic perspective to this co-authored memoir, seamlessly intertwining his experiences as an openly gay man from the United States with the rich traditions of the Gohil dynasty. Beyond his royal connections, Duke DeAndre is a fervent advocate for LGBTQIA+ rights, utilizing his influential platform to amplify diverse voices. As the owner of H1927 LLC, he not only adds a layer of contemporary flair to the memoir but also contributes to the narrative with his expertise in beauty, fashion, and creative direction. Duke DeAndre is not just limited to his roles; he passionately engages in pop-up fashion shows, skillfully blending fashion with challenging conversations on human rights and sexual diversity. His commitment to love, activism, and inclusivity not only permeates the pages of the memoir but also extends to his innovative endeavors in fashion, where he showcases the latest offerings from H1927tmR, his private fashion label. Together, the co-authors weave a narrative that transcends borders and breaks barriers, inviting readers into a world where tradition and modernity converge, advocating for a future where everyone can embrace their true selves. *A Royal Commitment: Ten Years of Marriage and Activism* reflects their commitment to a more inclusive world, where love knows no boundaries.

A Call To Action

Call to Action:

Dear Readers,

As you close the final pages of *A Royal Commitment: Ten Years of Marriage and Activism*, we invite you to embark on your own journey towards a more inclusive and compassionate world. The stories within these pages are not just about the experiences of HRH Prince Manvendra Singh Gohil and HH Prince DeAndre Duke of Hanumanteshwar but are a testament to the enduring power of love, resilience, and advocacy.

Now, it's your turn. Here's how you can make a difference:

1. **Embrace Diversity:** Celebrate the uniqueness in yourself and others. Stand up against prejudice and discrimination, fostering an environment where everyone can be their authentic selves.

2. **Advocate for Change:** Use your voice to challenge societal norms and push for inclusivity. Advocate for LGBTQIA+ rights, challenge stereotypes, and promote understanding.

3. **Support LGBTQIA+ Organizations:** Contribute your time, resources, or support to organizations working towards LGBTQIA+ rights and well-being. Every action, no matter how small, makes a difference.

4. **Engage in Difficult Conversations:** Break down barriers by engaging in open, honest, and respectful conversations about human rights, love, and diversity. Challenge misconceptions and promote understanding.

5. **Educate Yourself:** Stay informed about LGBTQIA+ history, rights, and current issues. Knowledge is a powerful tool in breaking down stereotypes and fostering acceptance.

6. **Spread Love:** In your personal and professional life, prioritize love, acceptance, and inclusivity. Create spaces where everyone feels valued and embraced.

A Royal Commitment is not just a memoir; it's an invitation to be a part of a broader movement towards a world where love knows no boundaries. Your commitment to change can be a catalyst for a more compassionate and understanding society.

Thank you for joining us on this journey.

With love,

HRH Prince Manvendra Singh Gohil and HH Prince DeAndre, Duke of Hanumanteshwar

Stay In Touch With Us

H1927llc.com
FB H1927
FB A Royal Commitment Ten Years of Marriage and Activism
FB The Gay Royals
FB Manvendra Singh Gohil
FB Duke DeAndre Richardson

Instagram
@Hanumanteshwar1927tm
@princemanvendrasgohil
@duke.hanumanteshwar

LinkedIn
Manvendra Singh Gohil
Duke Hanumanteshwar

X
@PrinceRajpipla
@DukeDeAndre

Tribel
@duke1927

The B Corp Movement

Dear reader,

Thank you for reading this book and joining the Publish Your Purpose community! You are joining a special group of people who aim to make the world a better place.

What's Publish Your Purpose About?

Our mission is to elevate the voices often excluded from traditional publishing. We intentionally seek out authors and storytellers with diverse backgrounds, life experiences, and unique perspectives to publish books that will make an impact in the world.

Beyond our books, we are focused on tangible, action-based change. As a woman—and LGBTQ+—owned company, we are committed to reducing inequality, lowering levels of poverty, creating a healthier environment, building stronger communities, and creating high-quality jobs with dignity and purpose.

As a Certified B Corporation, we use business as a force for good. We join a community of mission-driven companies building a more equitable, inclusive, and sustainable global economy. B Corporations must meet high standards of transparency, social, and environmental performance, and accountability as determined by the nonprofit B Lab. The certification process is rigorous and ongoing (with a recertification requirement every three years).

How Do We Do This?

We intentionally partner with socially and economically disadvantaged businesses that meet our sustainability goals. We embrace and encourage our authors and employee's differences in race, age, color, disability, ethnicity, family or marital status, gender identity or expression, language, national origin, physical and mental ability, political affiliation, religion, sexual orientation, socio-economic status, veteran status, and other characteristics that make them unique.

Community is at the heart of everything we do—from our writing and publishing programs to contributing to social enterprise nonprofits like reSET (www.resetco.org) and our work in founding B Local Connecticut.

We are endlessly grateful to our authors, readers, and local community for being the driving force behind the equitable and sustainable world we are building together.

To connect with us online or publish with us, visit us at www.publishyourpurpose.com.

Elevating Your Voice,

Jenn T Grace

Jenn T. Grace
Founder, Publish Your Purpose